EXPLORING
Door County

To Julie,
who shares my pack,
inspires my dreams,
and deeply loves
this Peninsula, named
Door

EXPLORING
Door County

Craig Charles

NORTHWORD PRESS

Minnetonka, Minnesota

© Craig Charles, 1999

Photography ©: George R. Cassidy/Third Coast, 20; Craig Charles, front cover inset photos, back cover, 31, 59, 142, 163; David L. Denemark/Third Coast, 95; Ken Dequaine, 66, 126, 158, 198, 203; Sue Hagen/Third Coast, 186; Brent Nicastro, 77, 109; Todd V. Phillips/Third Coast 102, 218; Beth Quade, 116; Willard Romantini, 183; John Touscany/Third Coast, 38; Ken Wardius/Third Coast, 165; Zane Williams, front cover photo; Wisconsin Department of Tourism Development, 10, 54, 148, 191

NorthWord Press
5900 Green Oak Drive
Minnetonka, MN 55343
1-800-328-3895

Cover design by Russell Kuepper
Book design by Moonlit Ink
Map Art by Donna Frankenberg

Charles, Craig
    Exploring Door County / Craig Charles.
        p. cm.
    ISBN 1-55971-681-9
    1. Door County (Wis.)--Guidebooks. I. Title.
  F587.D7C47 1999
  917.75'630443--dc21

Printed in Malaysia

PREFACE

Door County captured my interest at an early age. It lured me away from my Peninsula State Park campsite and hid me in a cedar forest, much to the dismay of park rangers searching for this lost seven-year-old. The peninsula hasn't lost its grip.

Today, the lakeshore waves that pound Door County crest beneath my sea kayak, and the peninsula's quaint country roads disappear beneath the tires of my bicycle. Its forests still shelter my hiking boots from a world of rapid transit while its beautiful beaches provide a welcome pillow of sand on a lazy summer day.

Recently, my wife and I have begun traipsing Door County with our two-year-old son, Benjamine. To Ben, the peninsula is an endless land of croaking frogs and buckets of sand. His innocence encourages me and his curiosity inspires me to press on ever farther.

This guide will take you off Door County's well-traveled paths into a world of secluded beaches, isolated campsites and deserted country roads. You'll be encouraged to stroll, backpack, pedal, ski and paddle to experience Door County at its natural best.

But the Door Peninsula is a fragile place–a delicate balance of rock, lake and land that demands special consideration and protection. Now, the responsibility for this constant vigilance is in your hands, because you've just begun *Exploring Door County*.

Symbol Key

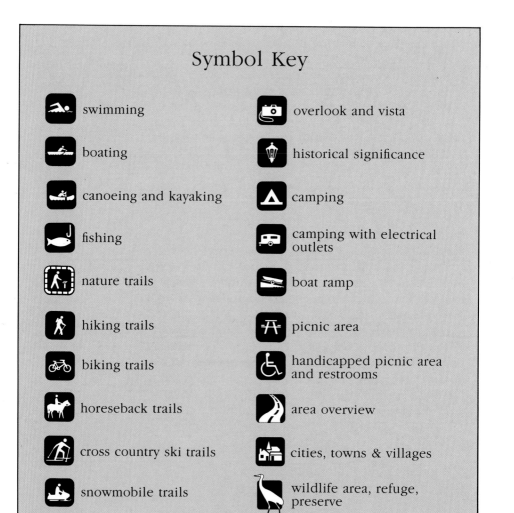

swimming

boating

canoeing and kayaking

fishing

nature trails

hiking trails

biking trails

horeseback trails

cross country ski trails

snowmobile trails

overlook and vista

historical significance

camping

camping with electrical outlets

boat ramp

picnic area

handicapped picnic area and restrooms

area overview

cities, towns & villages

wildlife area, refuge, preserve

TABLE OF CONTENTS

INTRODUCTION 11

SOUTHERN DOOR COUNTY 21
Through the Windshield 22
Potawatomi State Park 28
Wequiock Falls County Park 39
Red Banks Historic Wayside 39
Bayshore County Park 39
Red River County Park 40
Chaudoir's Dock County Park 40
Haines Town Park 40
Tornado Memorial Park 41
Sugar Creek County Park 41
Gardner Town Park 41
Claflin Memorial County Park 41
Idlewild Town Park 43
Forestville Dam County Park 43
Robert La Salle County Park 43
Clay Banks Town Park 44
Sturgeon Bay Canal Town Park 44
Portage Town Park 44
Gardner Swamp Wildlife Area 45
Beaches 47
The Ahnapee State Trail 49
The Ice Age Trail 51
Bicycle Tours 52
Canoe and Kayak Routes 56
Cities, Towns and Villages 58
    Sturgeon Bay 58
    Brussels .64

BAYSHORE 67
Through the Windshield 68
Peninsula State Park 80
Frank E. Murphy County Park 99
Harbor View Village Park 99
Egg Harbor Village Park 99

BAYSHORE cont.

Egg Harbor Nature Area .100
Fish Creek Community Center Park 100
Sunset Town Park 100
Clark Park 100
Chambers Island Lighthouse Town Park 101
Anderson Dock 101
Sister Bay Village Park 101
Ellison Bluff County Park 101
Gateway Village Park 103
Ephraim Village Playground 103
Sister Bay Athletic Field 103
Ellison Bay Women's Club Park 103
Ellison Bay Men's Club Park 103
Fuller Tract Natural Area 104
Crossroads at Big Creek Historical
   and Environmental Preserve 105
Beaches 106
Bicycle Tours 108
Canoe and Kayak Routes 111
Cities, Towns and Villages 113
     Egg Harbor 113
     Fish Creek 115
     Ephraim 118
     Sister Bay 121
     Ellison Bay 123

LAKESHORE 127

Through the Windshield 128
Whitefish Dunes State Park 133
Newport State Park 138
Cave Point County Park 146
Schauer Town Park 146
Lakeside Town Park 146
Jacksonport Community Town Park 146
Meridian County Park 147
Lyle Harter-Matter Sanctuary 147
Baileys Harbor Recreation Field 147
Anclam Town Park 147
Baileys Harbor Fire Station Field 147
Baileys Harbor Ridges County Park 149

Boes Town Park 149
Town of Liberty Grove School Forest 149
Sand Bay Town Park .149
Europe Bay Town Park 150
Kangaroo Lake 150
Shivering Sands 152
Mink River Estuary 153
Ridges Sanctuary 156
Toft Point Nature Conservancy 159
Mud Lake Wildlife Area 160
Baileys Harbor Natural Areas 162
Cana Island Lighthouse 166
Beaches 168
Bicycle Tours 170
Canoe and Kayak Routes 176
Cities, Towns and Villages 182
        Baileys Harbor .182
        Jacksonport 184

ISLANDS 187

Through the Windshield 188
Rock Island State Park 195
Grand Traverse Islands Park 200
Door Bluff Headlands County Park 204
Wisconsin Bay Town Park 204
Washington Island Athletic Field 204
Sand Dunes Town Park 204
Eastside County Park 204
Jackson Harbor Dunes Town Park 204
Schoolhouse Beach Town Park 205
Mountain Road Town Park 205
Jackson Harbor Ridges 205
Beaches 206
Bicycle Tours 208
Canoe and Kayak Routes 210
Cities, Towns and Villages 212
        Washington Island 212
        Gills Rock 217
        Northport 219

EPILOGUE: The Future 220

INTRODUCTION

The Door Peninsula is a land of striking natural beauty, rich in ethnic heritage and cultural values. Door leads all other American counties in shoreline frontage with nearly 250 coastal miles on the surrounding waters of Lake Michigan and Green Bay. These waterways are part of a larger, more complex system that includes tributary lakes, streams, springs and wetlands.

Door County's overwhelming natural beauty is due largely to the geology of the region. Carved by glacial action, the county is part of a spectacular limestone peninsula that juts 80 miles into Lake Michigan. Known as the Niagara Escarpment, this limestone ledge is recognizable to travelers heading north from Green Bay enjoying the magnificent bayshore view. The escarpment forms the rugged backbone of the entire Door Peninsula and arcs through Canada over 900 miles to New York State, where it supports the plunging waters of Niagara Falls.

The terrain on the peninsula is sometimes gentle and forgiving, often wild and rugged. Rocky limestone cliffs give way to sandy beaches on the western shore of the peninsula, while verdant forests meet marshy bays on its eastern coast. Over 30 caves are known to exist in Door County, including Tecumseh, the longest cave in Wisconsin, near the village of Egg Harbor.

Door County leads the nation in its number of lighthouses but, despite these life-saving beacons, over 200 shipwrecks lie scattered along the Door Peninsula shoreline, providing an eerie grave for unfortunate mariners lost at sea. Many of those sailors met their demise in the treacherous passage at the tip of Door County known as Porte des Morts, or Death's Door. The county owes its name to this dangerous strait and even today modern visitors can still feel the danger felt by early sailors when at Gill's Rock the waters of Green Bay meet the waters of Lake Michigan in a violent clash of surf and spray. Today, ferries routinely shuttle both autos and passengers from the Door County mainland across Death's Door Strait to Washington Island in safety and comfort, but adventuresome sea kayakers

Oh, that glorious Wisconsin wilderness! Everything new and pure . . . Young hearts, young leaves, flowers, animals, the winds and the streams and the sparkling lakes all rejoicing together.
—John Muir

(opposite page)
Wind and waves combine to carve rugged sea caves from Door County's rocky lakeshore.

11

still challenge the passage as did the earliest mariners, with pack and paddle, keeping the legend alive.

Sandwiched by Green Bay to the west and Lake Michigan to the east, Door tops all other Wisconsin counties in parks and nature preserves. Adventurers will find over 100 miles of trails for hiking, biking and skiing. These maintained trails traverse five state parks, meander through nature preserves and skirt both rugged bluffs and sandy beaches.

The folks who live here are as varied as the terrain. The peninsula is an ethnic melting pot. Washington Island at the northern end of the county was settled by Icelanders, while the village of Brussels at the peninsula's southern end remains a stronghold of Belgian ancestry. A countywide census completed in the 1870s found settlers from Prussia, Bohemia, Ireland, Norway, Sweden, Denmark and Canada. Today bratwurst and beer are found at nearly every summer festival in the county, attesting to the strong German heritage that remains on this splendid peninsula.

The natural beauty of the area continues to draw artists, writers and craftspeople to its shores. Today these folks offer visitors a variety of cultural experiences, including dance, art, theater and literature, unsurpassed in America's heartland.

A 1914 publication of the United Fruit Growers Company touts Door County as the "California of the North." That may be stretching the truth a bit, but the fact of the matter is that the Door Peninsula does enjoy a climate somewhat better than its northern neighbors do. The village of Jacksonport lies on the 45th meridian, halfway between the North Pole and the Equator. Sandwiched by the waters of Lake Michigan to the east and Green Bay to the west, the peninsula is somewhat cushioned from winter's icy blasts and summer's scorching heat waves. However, temperatures on the peninsula can vary dramatically and visitors should carry a wide range of clothing.

The influence of Lake Michigan becomes most evident on those occasions when an eight-mile trip from the bay side of the peninsula to the lakeshore means a ten-degree temperature drop in summer.

12

During winter, lake-effect snowstorms have been known to drop ten inches of snow on the peninsula's lakeshore while the bay side receives only a dusting. This will come as good news to skiers since the lakeshore is blessed with some of the finest cross-country ski trails in mid-America.

Partly due to its climate, the Door Peninsula remains the third-largest cherry-producing area in the nation. It also produces 40% of Wisconsin's apple crop. May finds the fruit trees in bloom as an explosion of pink and white blossoms marks the beginning of the summer season. Mid- to late July is cherry-picking time and a great time to visit "cherryland."

You can get to Door County by air, land or water. Austin Straubel Field in Green Bay is served by many major airlines, including Northwest, United and American Airlines. Cherryland Airport in Sturgeon Bay is served by Alliance Airlines with daily flights to Chicago. Rental cars are available in Green Bay and Sturgeon Bay.

The city of Green Bay, Wisconsin, lies at the western base of the Door Peninsula, and most visitors pass through this industrial workhorse en route to Door County. Extending east of this city lies Wisconsin State Highway 29. For practical and geographical reasons this highway forms the imaginary base of the Door Peninsula as it meets the Lake Michigan shore in the picturesque coastal community of Kewaunee.

Visitors to Door County typically arrive via Interstate 43 from Milwaukee and Chicago, Highway 29 from Minneapolis–St. Paul and Highway 41-141 from the north country. These highways converge in Green Bay and continue into Door County via Highway 57.

If you're lost, the Door County Chamber of Commerce will give you directions. The phone is 920-743-4456.

You can cross Lake Michigan on a passenger-and-car ferry from Ludington, Michigan, to Manitowoc, Wisconsin. Summer seasonal service begins in mid-May. For schedule information, phone 800-253-0094.

Lodging facilities on the Door Peninsula range from rustic bayshore cottages to modern year-round motels complete with indoor pools, whirlpools and saunas.

MEET INCREASE CLAFLIN, PENINSULA PIONEER
Increase Claflin and his wife, Mary, became Door County's first permanent white settlers when they built a cabin at Little Sturgeon Bay in 1835. When other settlers broke Claflin's solitude, Increase moved up the Peninsula, becoming the first permanent white settler at the village that still bears the name he chose, Fish Creek.

13

THE COTTAGE LIFE

Most housekeeping units on the peninsula rent from Saturday to Saturday during the summer season. A few may rent for two- or three-night minimums, especially during fall, winter and spring.

Prices are seasonal, reaching a peak during the summer months and over the New Year holiday. Prices also depend on which village, town or city you wish to visit. In general, Sturgeon Bay offers the most affordable accommodations while Ephraim offers the most exclusive and expensive.

Bed-and-breakfast inns are gaining in popularity. A few of these establishments offer not only turn-of-the-century atmosphere, but modern amenities as well, including in-room whirlpools and showers. Some inns provide an opportunity to stay with the locals and get an insider's view of life on the peninsula.

Cottages remain the most popular and affordable lodging alternative for families. Many hotels and motels here do not allow children and pets, making cottages not only a pleasant alternative but a true necessity.

Since the early 1980s when visitors often found "no vacancy" signs on busy summer weekends, a hotel/motel/condominium construction boom has occurred. This has expanded both the number of beds and the variety of accommodations available. Some long-time visitors have complained about this construction boom, and developers are becoming sensitive to this criticism, building facilities that blend better with the landscape.

Despite increased lodging opportunities, reservations are still highly recommended to avoid disappointment. The best source for current information is the Door County Chamber of Commerce; phone: 920-743-4456, fax: 920-743-7873 or write them at Box 406, Sturgeon Bay, WI 54235. Tell the chamber where you'd like to stay, your budget limitations and what type of accommodations you're looking for, and they'll give you several options. The chamber also operates an extensive internet web site with a great deal of valuable information including lodging alternatives, vacancies and an updated calendar of events. Their web site address is http://www.doorcountyvacations.com. If you arrive at the chamber of commerce office in Sturgeon Bay without a reservation, you'll find a user-friendly "InnLine" computer monitor in a kiosk adjacent to the chamber office. This system provides 24-hour vacancy information and telephone connections.

Door County's five state parks harbor the priceless gems of the peninsula. Towering limestone cliffs meet clear blue waters at Peninsula State Park. Endangered plants anchor ancient sand dunes at Whitefish Dunes State Park. Cool Lake Michigan winds fan Rock Island State Park. Ruffed grouse explode from the verdant forest of Newport State Park, and white-tailed deer find shelter in the wooded hills of Potawatomi State Park.

Much of the natural beauty of the peninsula has been preserved in these state parks, as well as in county and town parks and nature preserves. These parks contain delicate and complex ecosystems harboring endangered plant communities. While the parks are designed for fun and relaxation, they require responsible camping to ensure their gifts for future generations.

The Door Peninsula is blessed with over 600 state park campsites for those wishing to pitch a tent, roll out a sleeping bag or wheel in a recreational vehicle.

Despite the encouraging number of campsites, a camping trip to one of the state parks requires prior planning and often advance reservations. This is the rule rather than the exception during June, July and August, and the second and third weekends in October when Egg Harbor and Sister Bay hosts its annual fall celebration. Plans are currently under way to accept telephone reservations for all Wisconsin State Parks through a centralized reservation system no more than 11 months prior to the date of arrival. For up-to-date information or to receive a free state park visitor guide and campsite reservation application, call 800-432-8747 or write: DNR Parks, Box 7921, Madison, WI 53707, e-mail: wiparks@dnr.state.wi.us. Additional information can also be found via the Internet at www.dnr. state.wi.us/org/land/parks. Private campground infor- mation may be obtained through the Door County Chamber of Commerce; phone: 920-743-4456.

If you plan to arrive by vehicle as most visitors do, you'll need a Wisconsin state park vehicle admission sticker. A vehicle admission sticker is not required to simply drive through the parks. However, if you park your car for any reason you'll have to pay the price of admission. Both daily and annual stickers are available,

LODGING, RETAIL AND RESTAURANTS
In 1980, there were 3,112 lodging rooms available in Door County. Today there are over 5,100. Nearly one-third of the restaurants and almost 40% of the retail stores opened after 1980.

Door County has five
state parks and one
state trail, more than
any other county in
the country.

and the nominal fees are higher for nonresidents. Brown, Kewaunee and Door counties all converge on the Door Peninsula, adding a variety of county parks to a visitor's travel agenda. Thoughtful individuals and conservation organizations, notably the Nature Conservancy and Ridges Sanctuary, Inc., have preserved the biological diversity of the peninsula within untamed sanctuaries open to the public.

Hiking trails on the peninsula vary from gentle, easy strolls to strenuous backcountry rambles. Wildlife is abundant, and those willing to walk an extra mile or rise an extra hour earlier are sometimes rewarded with a fleeting glimpse of a ruffed grouse in flight or a coyote on the prowl. And whether you're a once-a-year peddler or a weekend racer, you'll find bicycle routes to suit your style. Many of the trails recommended in this book have been designated bicycle routes by the Wisconsin Division of Tourism due to their scenic value and low traffic. Automobiles are outlawed on the Sunset Bicycle Trail and the Ahnapee State Trail. The other tours mapped, however, are regular county and state highways where you'll have to share the road with motor vehicles. Consideration on the part of both drivers and riders is necessary.

Quaint. Picturesque. Cozy. Historic. Door Peninsula communities have fought hard to avoid the blatant commercial tourist trappings that can plague vacation areas. Long providing a haven for artists, retirees and transplanted city folk, the people here are proud of their heritage and eager to preserve it. Visitors will find a festival nearly every weekend in the summer. Autumn brings visitors to enjoy the vibrant fall colors. Winter brings ice fishing derbies, cross-country ski races and hot buttered rum.

World-class fishing opportunities await anglers visiting the Door Peninsula. The variety of bottom structure, the diverse shoreline and the variety of fish species present outstanding fishing action. The Wisconsin Department of Natural Resources has been stocking fish in the waters surrounding the Door Peninsula for nearly 20 years. Today their efforts are being rewarded with a legendary fishery that includes chinook salmon, lake trout, walleye pike, northern pike, whitefish, bass and perch.

Visitors without the knowledge, equipment or experience to pursue Lake Michigan salmon and trout by themselves will find charter fishing guides the most effective means of getting to Lake Michigan's trophy fishery. To hook up with a charter captain call the Door County Chamber of Commerce at 920-743-4456.

If you're planning to board a Lake Michigan charter, bring a day pack with warm clothing even in mid-summer. Once you're on Lake Michigan, cool breezes will be blowing and it's nice to have the comfort of a wool sweater and down vest. Rain gear is also advised. You'll need a Wisconsin fishing license, too. A daily fishing license is available, but usually not from the charter captain, so pick one up before you arrive. Beverages are usually available on board but you're welcome to bring your own on most charters. You'll want a cooler to bring your fish home. The charter provides all your fishing gear and will fillet your catch.

The Wisconsin state-record chinook salmon, a 43-pound, 3-ounce monster, was caught aboard an Algoma-based charter boat by a visiting Minnesota angler in 1983. With luck, the next record could be yours!

Meanwhile, walleye enthusiasts are hopeful the next state record for that species is swimming in Green Bay waters off the city of Sturgeon Bay. Lunker walleyes by inland lake standards are routinely caught in Sawyer Harbor and many fish biologists predict the best is yet to come.

Visitors who prefer not to board a Lake Michigan charter can simply drop a worm off a dock or shore and hope for the best. Many bass, perch, northern pike, salmon and trout are caught from Door Peninsula public docks and piers each year by visitors who have invested no more than the price of a rod, reel and lure or live bait.

A canoe, sea kayak or runabout will open the waters to many fishing opportunities. Protected bays, inland lakes and vast stretches of open water provide plenty of chances to land the fish of a lifetime, so cast luck to the wind and hope for a pole bender.

MODEST DEVELOPMENT
Nearly 95% of Door County remains undeveloped. Development reaches its peak on the western shore of the peninsula, where planners are struggling to ensure that new construction is modest and environmentally sensitive.

"Sweet water seas" is how the French Jesuit missionaries of the 1600s described the salt-free Great Lakes as they paddled their canoes along exploration routes that included the Door Peninsula. Today, touring kayakers part these same inland seas, upholding the tradition and sharing an ageless adventure.

The Door Peninsula hosted Wisconsin's first American Canoe Association sea kayaking workshop in 1987. The Peninsula State Park location inspired rave reviews from paddlers attending from across the Great Lakes. The peninsula's back bays, pleasing promontories and calm-water coves welcome all levels of skill.

Canoeists heading for the peninsula can leave their river white-water equipment behind unless they plan on playing in the lakeshore surf. Canoeing opportunities on the peninsula do not include white-water rivers. Paddlers will not be disappointed, however. Secluded bays, inland lakes and even a fresh-water estuary rich in aquatic life greet visitors who arrive with canoes.

The peninsula has four inland lakes worthy of note for canoeists. Europe, Clark, Kangaroo and Mud lakes all afford public access with excellent canoeing opportunities. Inland lakes rarely prove threatening to canoeists and usually provide fishing opportunities to those wishing to wet their lines for panfish or the occasional northern pike or walleye.

Those looking for more challenging conditions will find open water paddling on both the bay side and lakeshore of the peninsula. Open-water crossings are discouraged in an open canoe unless the weather conditions, waves and paddlers' skills combine for a safe outing.

Protected bays and shoreline paddling opportunities are almost unlimited. As a rule, the bay side of the peninsula generally offers greater protection, warmer water and somewhat smaller breakers than the lakeshore. But rules are made to be broken, and canoeists and kayakers looking for a calm-water tour might consider heading to the lakeshore when waves are battering the bay side. Kayakers wishing to play in the surf will find beautiful breakers at Whitefish Dunes State Park and Portage Town Park. The waves really begin building in September and October when wet and dry suits become standard equipment. Paddlers can find open water at Northport year-round, but in winter most kayakers agree the Washington Island Ferry is the best way to cross the whitecaps.

The peninsula's beaches are pure delight for those eager to catch some rays after a long, cold Wisconsin winter. You'll find beaches that vary from vast rolling sand dunes to white slivers just large enough to keep the waves from licking your heels. A trip to the peninsula is just not complete unless you come home with a pocketful of sand whether you visit in July or January. Winter brings its own special rewards to beachcombers who often discover winter waves carving castles of ice.

The Door County Peninsula has been called one of the top ten cross-country ski areas in the nation, and this may well be the case when the snow is deep and the trails are groomed. Unfortunately, snowfall on the peninsula varies dramatically from year to year and even from bay side to lakeshore. Mid-January through mid-March usually provides the best conditions. Early and late-season skiers may wish to call the chamber of commerce information hotline prior to their visit: 920-743-4456 (ext. 3). The towering bluffs, the gorgeous views, the peaceful woodlands and the rolling fields are constants, however, and when winter cooperates they are unsurpassed.

Alpine skiers will find one ski area on the peninsula located at Potawatomi State Park. The slope has a moderate 120-foot vertical drop, but does boast a chair lift. Prices are reasonable.

Door County is a naturalist's delight. Whether you choose to make camp in southern Door County, on the Green Bay side or the lakeshore, or on one of the islands at the northern tip, you'll never be far from another adventure as you begin exploring the Door Peninsula.

ABUNDANT SHORELINE
Door County has more than 250 miles of shoreline. There are 92 public water access sites ranging from several miles, at state parks, to less than 100 feet at road endings.

SOUTHERN DOOR COUNTY

POTAWATOMI STATE PARK

IDLEWILD TOWN PARK

SAND BAY BEACH

HAINES TOWN PARK & BEACH

CLAFLIN MEMORIAL CTY. PARK

GARDNER TOWN PARK

GARDNER SWAMP WILDLIFE AREA

SUGAR CREEK CTY. PARK

CHAUDOIR'S DOCK CTY. PARK

SUNSET PARK BEACH

FRED J. PETERSON MEMORIAL POOL

OTUMBA PARK BEACH

PORTAGE TOWN PARK & BEACH

CANAL TOWN PARK BEACH

CLAY BANKS TOWN PARK

AHNAPEE STATE TRAIL

FORESTVILLE DAM CTY. PARK & BEACH

- RED RIVER CTY. PARK
- BAYSHORE CTY. PARK
- RED BANKS HISTORIC WAYSIDE
- WEQUIOCK FALLS CTY. PARK

▦ STATE PARKS
● TOWN, VILLAGE & COUNTY PARKS
▲ PRESERVES
■ BEACHES

Through the Windshield
AN OVERVIEW OF THE SOUTHERN DOOR

(overleaf)

A young angler tries
his luck off a Door
County pier.

Rolling hills, dairy farms, and bayshore vistas usher visitors into Door County. Once considered a stepping stone to points farther north, southern Door County is increasingly becoming a final destination for weary travelers. Captivated by its unpretentious rural atmosphere and reasonably priced shoreside accommodations, visitors are rediscovering this land once populated by Potawatomi and Winnebago Indians.

French explorers made many visits to southern Door County, taking advantage of its prominent location near the Fox-Wisconsin river watersheds and the Great Lakes trading routes. Today, visitors entering Door County via State Highway 57 arc across a geologic formation known as the Niagara Escarpment.

Wequiock Cascades County Park is an ideal location to take a close look at this rock outcropping. Here an exposed limestone ledge supports the tumbling water of Wequiock Creek. During the summer months this waterfall is little more than a trickle, but during spring runoff the flowing water creates a spectacular scene. Wequiock Creek terminates in a beautiful marsh as it enters Green Bay. This area, known as Point Au Sable, is prime waterfowl habitat. At low water this point offers beautiful white sand beaches accessible only by boat.

Continuing up the peninsula you'll get your first glimpse of the grand view overlooking a section of the Green Bay shore known as Red Banks. A historical marker and shoreside tablet here commemorate the visit of French explorer Jean Nicolet in 1634. Nicolet, an emissary of Governor Samuel de Champlain of New France, had been dispatched from Quebec to locate a convenient route to Asia. After paddling more than 1,000 miles through the Straits of Mackinac and on to Lake Michigan, Nicolet was convinced he had reached China. Landing on the Green Bay shore, Nicolet fully expected to meet the Chinese and had brought along an elaborate Oriental robe specifically for that occasion. Donning the robe and emerging from his canoe, Nicolet fired two pistols in the air, much to the amazement of the Winnebago Indians who had come to greet him. Fascinated by the "thunder" he carried in his hands, the Winnebagos treated Nicolet and his crew to a banquet of "six score beavers." Soon, however, it was to be the pelt of the beaver and not its appeal to the palate that would be prized by the white men who followed Nicolet.

Just north of Red Banks, situated atop the Niagara Escarpment, stands Bayshore County Park. This Brown County park (listed separately) affords breathtaking views of the waters of Green Bay and offers 83 campsites amidst a wooded setting. A boat launching ramp (fee) provides excellent access to fishermen seeking perch and walleye in Green Bay waters. A pier provides fishing opportunities for those without a boat to test their angling skills. Park management does not encourage swimming off the pier, but it's still a popular way to cool off on a warm summer day. Several spacious picnic areas are scattered throughout the park, complete with grills, picnic tables and a playground for children. A nature trail, softball diamond and shelter building combine to make Bayshore Park a popular spot for an hour or a weekend.

Continuing up the bayshore, travelers will encounter the Kewaunee County community of Dyckesville. Residents of Belgian ancestry continue to celebrate the "Kermiss" here on the third Sunday in September, celebrating the harvest as they have for more than 75 years. Fishermen commonly frequent this bayshore village to stock up on bait, tackle and supplies for perch fishing. While the village itself lacks adequate public access to Green Bay waters, it is surrounded by a pair of county parks with public boat-launching facilities. The second of these parks is Red River County Park, just north of the village. The Red River flows through this seven-acre park into Green Bay and includes 500 feet of bayshore frontage. A 40-foot summer "port-a-pier" and two boat-launching ramps provide access to the bay. The Red River supports a substantial smelt run in the spring, and dipping for the

CHERRYLAND BLOSSOMS

Door County has been called "cherryland" because it is the third largest cherry-producing area in the nation. White cherry blossoms begin making their appearance in mid-May, followed by pink apple blossoms a week later.

THE
PESHTIGO FIRE

silvery fish is a popular evening activity when the "run" is on.

Crossing the Door County line, visitors will pass through the 3,500-acre Belgian settlements of Namur and Brussels (listed separately). These settlements represent the largest rural concentration of Belgian-Americans in the United States. Due to the unique architecture of the 261 homes, barns, churches and chapels that dot the landscape, this settlement was listed on the National Register of Historic Places in 1989 and subsequently upgraded as a national Historic Landmark in 1991.

These Belgian immigrants built with locally gathered wood, brick and stone. The most striking building material visible from the highway is the red brick that often covers a framework of wooden logs. The brick was used in response to a tremendous fire which engulfed this community in the fall of 1871. The fire first began on the opposite side of Green Bay in the Peshtigo area, charring over 2,400 acres and claiming 800 lives before the inferno jumped the waters of Green Bay.

North of the village of Brussels, a wayside park established by Door County in 1927 marks the location where 57 pioneers perished. The villagers had sought refuge from the horrible inferno in an open field but were unable to escape the tremendous blaze. Nearby stands a well site that served as the last place of refuge for seven individuals attempting to escape the unbearable heat. The last man to crawl into the well pulled a wet blanket over the opening. Five of the seven desperate pioneers survived.

With the assistance of relatives from southern Wisconsin, the Belgian community rebuilt their shattered lives with fireproof brick, native fieldstone and wills of iron.

West of Brussels, a pair of county parks provides boaters with access to Green Bay. Fishermen will find an upgraded boat launch at Sugar Creek County Park (listed separately) and an emergency harbor of refuge for small boats at Chaudoir's Dock County Park (listed separately). Gardner Swamp Wildlife Area (listed

**THE
PESHTIGO FIRE**
The Peshtigo fire, which leapt the waters of Green Bay to kindle the forests of southern Door County, actually claimed more lives than the highly publicized Chicago Fire. Due to the isolation of the Door Peninsula, however, the Chicago Fire captured the nation's attention, and the suffering of peninsula pioneers went largely unnoticed.

separately) provides a nesting and resting location for both migratory and local waterfowl populations. This 1,000-acre preserve is open to the public year-round and provides opportunities for hiking, hunting, waterfowl observation and snowmobiling.

Visitors entering Door County via Highway 42 on the scenic Lake Michigan shoreline route will pass through the quaint Kewaunee County harbor communities of Kewaunee and Algoma, where it's easy to find a charter fishing captain anxious to add a passenger to his boat. Kewaunee takes its name from a Potawatomi Indian word meaning "we are lost." Apparently Indians paddling Lake Michigan would occasionally become disoriented amidst the deep fog on the lake while attempting to make their way back to shore. By shouting "Kewaunee" they alerted their friends on shore that they were lost and in need of direction. Today, Kewaunee's modern harbor employs sophisticated navigational equipment to aid recreational boaters during their lakeshore outings.

In the 1830s, an unknown explorer discovered what he thought was gold at the mouth of the Kewaunee River. The ensuing "gold fever" didn't quite pan out and Kewaunee settled into a lumber economy. Today, gold of a different sort is being collected from the Kewaunee River. In 1990, the Wisconsin Department of Natural Resources developed a new facility to collect and raise coho salmon and steelhead (rainbow) trout in the Kewaunee River. Spring and autumn are the best times to visit this fish collection facility in the scenic valley of the Kewaunee River. This is when trout and salmon make their upstream spawning runs from Lake Michigan. Once at the facility the large fish are directed up a fish ladder into collection ponds. Two large viewing windows allow visitors to glance under the water's surface to witness the powerful fish, driven by primordial instincts, jumping the ladder into the collection pools. These fish are then used to stock Lake Michigan, adding to its trophy fishery.

Evidence of the steelhead stocking program's success is mounting. In 1997, while trolling off Algoma with her uncle, Minnesota angler Debbie Morrison

LIGHT KEEPER'S LOVE

Lighthouse keeper William Cochems and his wife tended the Sherwood Point Lighthouse for over 30 years. Following his wife's death in 1929, Cochems built a small monument in her honor near the lighthouse. The marker still stands as a monument to a love shared between the keepers of a light on a lonely peninsula.

landed a state-record steelhead (rainbow) trout weighing 27.11 pounds.

More than just trophy fish await visitors to Algoma, the site of another former Potawatomi Indian village. Crescent Beach, a one-half-mile-long public ribbon of sand, lines the harbor of Algoma, inviting visitors to lay out a beach blanket or drop in a sea kayak. The handicapped-accessible Crescent Beach Boardwalk connects the city's impressive Visitor Center with Algoma's municipal marina. The boardwalk, its vista platforms and benches were built by volunteers and are constructed entirely of recycled plastic.

This city's public harbor has undergone extensive renovation, including additional docking facilities. Algoma's striking red North Pierhead Lighthouse is one of the city's most prominent, and photographed, features. The light station began operating in 1932 when it replaced a wooden tower light that dated back to 1893.

Algoma's pier is unique, since it was constructed in two sections to allow an opening in the concrete for the exit of water in rough seas. This opening required that a steel "catwalk" be constructed above the watery gap to allow a lighthouse keeper to reach the light station.

Named "Wolf River" by early settlers, the town's name reverted to its Indian name, Ah-na-pee, meaning gray wolf, in 1859. By 1897 the town had grown to 1,700. Then the name was changed to Algoma, or "Park of Flowers." Sometimes referred to as "Penguin City," Algoma enjoys a summer climate substantially cooler than its northern neighbors, due to the chilling influence of Lake Michigan.

From Algoma, travelers with additional leisure time can continue north on County Trunk S along the lakeshore to County Trunk U. Frenchman Robert La Salle followed this route by canoe, camping on the southern Door lakeshore in 1679 before establishing a fur trading post on Rock Island. Robert La Salle County Park (listed separately) commemorates La Salle's visit and provides visitors with both shoreside access to Lake Michigan and a convenient picnicking location.

FISH STORIES
Algoma continues its tradition as Lake Michigan's record-setting fishing harbor. In 1996 Bob Wenker of White Bear Lake, Minnesota, broke an 18-year-old record by hauling in a 35.11-pound brown trout. Remarkably, that record was broken just 25 days later when Algoma resident Lloyd Arndt cranked in a brown that weighed just 1/100 of a pound more.

West of La Salle County Park, on Highway J near Highway 42, Forestville Dam County Park (listed separately) provides canoe access to the slow-moving Ahnapee River. The Forestville Pond was formed by damming a portion of the Ahnapee during the late 1800s to provide hydro power for a gristmill. Frequently choked by aquatic weeds, the pond today does not provide the swimming and fishing opportunities it once did. Nevertheless, canoeists anxious to "lily dip" a paddle will enjoy the pond, and the area provides excellent access for mountain bikers wishing to shorten their ride on the Ahnapee State Trail.

State Highways 42 and 57 converge south of Sturgeon Bay near the access road to Potawatomi State Park. This forested preserve offers a modern 125-unit campground and opportunities for fishing, hiking, biking, skiing and sight-seeing. Potawatomi offers the only downhill ski area on the peninsula, and an observation tower there provides an outstanding panorama of Sturgeon Bay and points beyond.

Arriving in Sturgeon Bay, one can see from this community's relatively large size why it remains the center of government, commerce and industry in Door County. Viewing its excellent harbor from one of the two bridges that span the bay, it's easy to visualize the attraction this area held for nineteenth-century lumbermen anxious to harvest its virgin timber.

Father James Marquette was the first white man to record stopping at what is now Sturgeon Bay, in 1673. Following a portage trail blazed by the resident Indians, Father Marquette carried his canoe across the strip of land separating Green Bay from Lake Michigan. Today such a portage is no longer necessary. A ship canal, dredged in 1878 at the insistence of lumbermen, created a navigable channel uniting the waters of Green Bay and Lake Michigan at Sturgeon Bay.

KEWAUNEE LIGHTHOUSE
Kewaunee's South Pierhead Light was constructed in 1909 as a fog signal. In 1931 an upper wood frame section was added to the original steel building to house a Fresnel lighthouse lens. This lighthouse replaced a pair of range lights that had been in place on the pier since 1891.

STATE PARKS

Potawatomi State Park

Approximately three miles south of the city of Sturgeon Bay, turn north off Hwy 42-57 onto Park Drive. Travel approximately two miles, crossing County C, to the park entrance on the east side of Park Drive. Address: 3740 Park Drive, Sturgeon Bay, WI 54235. Phone: 920-746-2890.

FACILITIES:

123 campsites with electricity at 23 sites. Showers are available. Reservable handicapped-accessible cabin with full facilities available. Reservations are recommended during summer although 20 percent of the campsites are kept available on a first-come, first-served basis. Open year-round.

RECREATION:

Hiking trails, fishing spots, downhill ski hill, cross-country ski trails, snowmobile trails, observation tower, boat ramp and biking opportunities.

A rugged, forested Green Bay shoreline greets visitors to Potawatomi State Park. Limestone cliffs give way to a rocky bayshore, and tall pine and birch trees sway in the wind.

Located as it is on the western edge of the city of Sturgeon Bay, Potawatomi State Park combines the convenience of city life with the isolation of a 1,200-acre forest preserve. The park lies midway between the city of Green Bay, at the base of the Door Peninsula, and the village of Gills Rock, at the tip of Door County.

Many visitors to Potawatomi arrive in hopes of hooking a world-class walleye from the waters that surround the park. Others enjoy the spectacular vista from the observation platform that towers over the park. Bicyclists will find Potawatomi a convenient starting point for their further exploration of Door County. In fact, long-range park plans call for the development of a bicyclist camp for touring riders both here and at Newport State Park on the northern tip of the peninsula, although there has been no progress at turning this plan into reality.

Day hikers will enjoy the wildflowers and admire the white birch and red pine stands that provide cover for wildlife and renewal for trail trampers.

The park takes its name from the Potawatomi Indians who roamed this land when Jean Nicolet recorded a visit here in 1634. They called themselves BO-DE-WAD-ME, which means "keeper of the fire." The term was often mispronounced and eventually was written and adopted as Potawatomi. Sharing this land with the Potawatomi were other Woodland Indians, including the Fox, Chippewa, Menominee, Sauk and Winnebago tribes. Native populations survived into the early 1800s, but gradually declined as white settlers staked their claims on the Door Peninsula.

The prominent limestone headland at the mouth of Sturgeon Bay above which the observation tower now stands has historically been known as Government Bluff. In 1834, the federal government began a rock quarry here, and Government Bluff was recognized not only for its commanding strategic view of both the Sturgeon Bay and Green Bay coastlines, but also for the high-quality limestone found beneath the shallow soil. In 1837, a 1,000-acre reservation was established on the site, serving to isolate this area, much to the dismay of those early settlers who coveted both the natural and aesthetic resources of Government Bluff.

In 1928, the state of Wisconsin took an interest in the property and purchased the 1,046 acres at the mouth of Sturgeon Bay known as Government Bluff for $1.25 an acre. It was then given the name "Nicolet State Park," in honor of explorer Jean Nicolet who was thought to have passed through Sawyer Harbor in 1634. It became the thirteenth property established as a state park.

In November of 1928, State Conservation Director Louis Nagler asked the people of Sturgeon Bay to suggest a different name for the newly created park. The local chamber of commerce passed a resolution that the park be named "Potawatomi" in honor of the Indian tribe native to the area, and the resolution passed.

HOME AND GARDEN WALK
Each July the Door County Hospital Auxiliary hosts a "home and garden walk" to highlight homes or buildings of particular interest or historical value. Contact the Door County Memorial Hospital (920-743-5566) for information.

One year later a road was constructed through the "Daisy Field," up the bluff and around Sawyer Harbor. This road today is known as Shore Road, which turns into Norway Road as you approach the tower.

In 1931, The Sawyer Commercial Club requested permission to erect an observation tower at Potawatomi, similar to the tower located at Peninsula State Park in northern Door County. Permission was granted, and construction was begun on August 14, 1931, and completed just 51 days later. Today, when you stand atop 150-foot-high Government Bluff on top of this 75-foot-high observation tower, you are 225 feet above the waters of Green Bay. The view provides a sweeping panorama of Sawyer Harbor, the waters of Green Bay and beyond.

POTAWATOMI
STATE PARK

(opposite page)

A small creek meanders through a garden of marsh marigolds en route to its outlet at Lake Michigan.

30

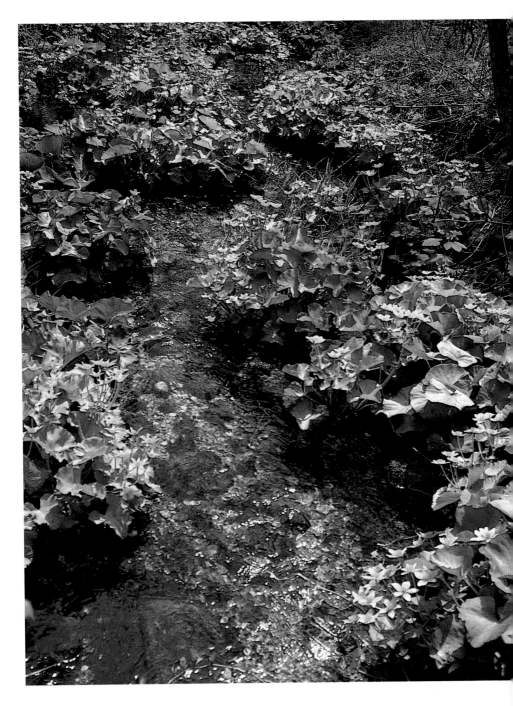

Today, visitors may be treated to a serenade from the more than fifty species of songbirds known to nest in or near the park. Hikers will find the dense forest filled with red oak, sugar maple, basswood and paper birch trees. Along the cliffs, white cedars are common. Spring is the best season for a wildflower hike, but many species will still be in bloom during the summer and fall as well. White-tailed deer are commonly sighted, and raccoons, gray squirrels, opossums and chipmunks will be happy to treat themselves to your food cache if it's left unprotected.

DAISY FIELD
CAMPGROUND

Potawatomi State Park is also the eastern terminus of the Ice Age National Scenic Trail, which begins at the observation tower on Government Bluff. This 1,000-mile-long trail follows the edge of the farthest advance of the Wisconsin Glacier across the state. It dips southward from Door County before looping north and west to the banks of the St. Croix River. Although unfinished, the first part of the trail begins at the observation tower and follows Tower Trail through Potawatomi Park south along the shoreline and exits the park off Shore Road. Ice Age Trail symbols will guide hikers. The next major link in the trail occurs along the Ahnapee State Trail, which follows an abandoned railroad grade 15 miles to Algoma, Wisconsin. The connection between the park and the Ahnapee State Trail is not complete, but hikers can check with park rangers for the most convenient link.

Potawatomi State Park serves about 200,000 visitors annually. No doubt that number will increase now that shower facilities at the park's Daisy Field Campground are provided. This will also increase competition for the park's 123 campsites; reservations, especially for summer weekend campers, will become a necessity. Since 80% of the park's campsites are reservable, visitors arriving without a reservation, especially mid-week, may still have a shot at securing a campsite for the evening. When making reservations, keep in mind that all campsites in the south loop and odd-numbered campsites in the north loop of Daisy Field Campground are reservable. When the "no vacancy" sign is posted, you can have your name placed on a waiting list and play the campground shuffle. This requires that you meet at park headquarters the following morning at 10 A.M. At that time campsites are reassigned and campsite vacancies filled.

Potawatomi State Park is one of three state parks in Wisconsin to offer a handicapped-accessible cabin, available by advance reservation. New in 1995, this modern facility is located in the Daisy Field campground and known as the "cabin by the bay." It accommodates up to six persons but at least one must be handicapped.

SHERWOOD POINT LIGHTHOUSE
Sherwood Point and its Coast Guard lighthouse take their name from Door Peninsula settler Peter Sherwood. Sherwood settled on the point in 1836, remaining until his death at the age of 80, in 1862. The Sherwood Point Lighthouse, situated on a bluff overlooking Sturgeon Bay, was built in 1883. The grounds are no longer open to the public except during the annual Door County Maritime Museum Lighthouse Walk held the third weekend in May.

After you set up camp, it's time to plan activities. Potawatomi offers a variety of interpretive programs for all ages. A naturalist might give a program about the animals or plant life in the park, or discuss the history or geology of the area. Programs are offered during June, July and August and are a good starting point for your exploration of the park. Check at the park office or on the park bulletin boards for times and places.

The steeps cliffs and clear waters of Potawatomi make it a favorite oasis for day hikers as well as campers. Its proximity to the largest community on the peninsula make the trails attractive to local residents and visitors alike. The park is open year-round and many of the trails double as cross-country ski routes in the winter months.

HIKING TRAILS

Tower Trail: The trailhead for the Tower Trail (3.5 miles) is reached by driving to the parking area atop the Potawatomi ski hill. This vantage provides a view of Green Bay waters to the north and rolling countryside to the west. Follow the trail north on the paved roadway along the highest bluff in the park to the observation tower. Once atop the tower, you'll be 225 feet above Sawyer Harbor, a popular year-round fishing spot. The trail continues south down a forested bluff to the shore of Sturgeon Bay. From here you'll wind through a cedar archway before making the gentle climb back to the trailhead.

Hemlock Trail: Pick up the Hemlock Trail (2.5 miles) at parking lot 2 off Shore Road. The trail follows the service road to the picnic area along the shores of Sturgeon Bay, where fishermen are often spotted trolling for walleye pike, bass or trout. Crossing Shore Road, the trail bends north along the north side of the campground. After crossing Norway Road, you will approach a field where summer brings the blooms of common St. Johns-wort. Crossing Norway Road a second time, you'll be hiking the interior of the

POISON IVY
Poison ivy is found throughout Door County, especially in disturbed areas near the lakeshore. It appears as a small plant, a creeping vine or a shrub. It has a woody stem and is known by its three-leaf groupings. The oil present in all parts of the plant causes irritation, inflammation, itching and swelling to many of those exposed. First aid includes removing all contaminated clothing and washing the exposed area with soap. Calamine lotion will soothe the skin where a rash develops.

forested park before cresting a limestone bluff and heading back down to Shore Road and the trailhead.

Ancient Shores Nature Trail: Ancient Shores Nature Trail is a half-mile, self-guided route that begins across from the service area at the center of the park. The trail's 25 stations describe the plant and animal life as well as the geology and geography of the park. The trail takes its name from the two glacial lakes that once covered portions of the park, including what is now the Daisy Field Campground.

CROSS-COUNTRY SKI TRAILS

In winter, cross-country skiers can experience the same varied terrain and views of Sturgeon Bay on 13 miles of groomed trails. The trails are generally quite easy although there are a few hairpin turns that beginners may wish to avoid. The park is open year-round with a few campsites available for those willing to brave the elements.

The **red trail** (3 miles) is an easy-stride-only park favorite. The trail takes skiers along the highest bluff at Potawatomi before descending a gradual but exciting slope back to the Nordic warming shelter. En route you will pass the 75-foot-high observation tower, but the tower is not maintained by the park for winter use. Cresting the bluff you'll have a view of Sawyer Harbor below and, if you're tall enough, on a clear day you might see Menominee, Michigan, 18 miles away.

The stride or skate-ski **black loop** (4.8 miles) gives skiers a chance to experience the northern half of Potawatomi Park. Beginning at the warming shelter near the picnic area you'll follow the red trail before heading off on a one-way trail through the forest. This is a nice spot to decide whether you've got the time and energy to continue the extra 1.3 miles of the red loop. If not, you'll descend to the camp area and the winter warming shelter.

The gentle **blue loop** (3 miles) has also been widened to an eight-foot corridor affording opportunities for either stride or skate skiing on the same track. Beginning at the Nordic warming shelter near the picnic area, the blue trail follows the bayshore before creeping along the southwest side of the Daisy Field Campground. As you descend along the limestone bluff, use caution as you make the final approach to Shore Road and the warming shelter.

The stride-only **green loop** (2.64 miles) shortens the blue loop but still provides skiers with a scenic and interesting trail. Begin by following the bayshore briefly before connecting with the blue loop along the limestone bluff that circles back to Shore Road and the parking area.

DOWNHILL SKIING

Downhill and telemark skiers eager to stretch their muscles will find a modest 120-foot drop at Potawatomi State Park. The three runs cater to beginners and experts alike with a double chair lift and two rope tows. A warming chalet offers a fireplace, snack bar and conversation with locals.

For more than 40 years, the entire operation at Mount Potawatomi has been run by the nonprofit Potawatomi Park Ski Club. These dedicated volunteers keep lift tickets affordable even for large families. The ski hill's chairlift and snow-making equipment were brought to Door County from a Northern Michigan ski hill by ski club volunteer Don Baudhuin, a Sturgeon Bay businessman. Just weeks before the chairlift was to be put into operation, Baudhuin suffered a fatal heart attack while on a helicopter-drop ski trip to British Columbia.

Today the snowmaking equipment Baudhuin was instrumental in securing helps keep the hill operating even during periods of only moderate snowfall. A brass plate on the hill's chairlift dedicates the lift to his memory.

Mount Potawatomi is open Saturdays, Sundays and holidays from 10:30 A.M. to 4:30 P.M. Lighted slopes allow night skiing each Wednesday from 6 to 10 P.M., weather permitting. For updated information and the

VOLUNTEER
CAMPGROUND
HOSTS
Peninsula and
Potawatomi state parks
participate in
Wisconsin's Volunteer
Campground Host
program. In exchange
for greeting campers,
passing out brochures
and performing minor
maintenance,
Campground Hosts
receive free camping
and vehicle admission.
The program requires
a four-week stint.
Applications are
available at the park
offices.

price of lift tickets call the ski area: 920-743-7033, or
Potawatomi State Park: 920-746-2890. To get to the
downhill ski area, exit Highway 57 south of Sturgeon
Bay at Park Road. Follow the signs to Potawatomi State
Park, but pass the park entrance and turn left (north)
on Olson Road. Take Olson Road to Gitchee Gummee
Road heading north to the ski area entrance. A state
park vehicle admission sticker is not required to park
at the downhill ski area.

POTAWATOMI
WINTER TRAILS

TOWN, VILLAGE
AND COUNTY PARKS

Wequiock Falls County Park (2 acres)

Located on Highway 57 at the southern end of the peninsula, this wayside park is situated on the Niagara Escarpment. Wequiock Creek cascades over the "ledge" in the spring, but slows to a trickle in the summer. Picnic tables and grates are provided, along with a first-hand look at the geologic formations that shape the peninsula.

Red Banks Historic Wayside (1 acre)

Located on Highway 57 north of Wequiock Falls, there stands a historic wayside paying tribute to Jean Nicolet, the first white man to land on the Green Bay shore, at a place called Red Banks. A bronze statue off the highway recalls Nicolet's visit. The wayside provides an excellent panorama of Green Bay waters.

Bayshore (Brown) County Park (92 acres)

The entrance is 15 miles north of Green Bay on Highway 57 and is well marked. Address: Route 1, New Franken, WI 54229. Phone: 920-866-2414.

FACILITIES:

There are 85 campsites, all available on a first-come, first-served basis. Water and flush toilets are operational about May 1, but pit toilets are available year-round. A camping fee is charged and there is a 14-day camping limit. Coin showers are available, and all campsites have electricity. Additionally, there is a laundry and a dumping station. No admission fee.

RECREATION:

The park has a boat ramp (with launch fee), and there are short hiking and cross-country ski trails. An outstanding view of Green Bay from the Niagara Escarpment and a spectacular descent to the park's boat landing make Bayshore Park a pleasant resting place for travelers. This park attracts fishing enthusiasts who launch their boats here in search of yellow perch.

(opposite page)
A cross-country skier in full stride tackles a Door County trail.

MYSTERY OF
THE *GRIFFIN*
In 1679 the 45-ton
sailing ship *Griffin*,
laden with valuable
furs, departed
Washington Island
under favorable skies.
Armed with seven
small cannons to
discourage unfriendly
Indians or the
occasional Great Lakes
pirate, the ship was en
route to Montreal. It
never arrived. Lost in a
storm? Captured by
pirates? Sunk by
Indians? No one
knows.

Several spacious picnic areas are scattered throughout the park for those wishing to grill some burgers while the children enjoy the playground. Nature trails, a baseball diamond, a volleyball area and a horseshoe pit also provide recreational opportunities. A shelter house on the park grounds may be rented year-round. The shelter has a fireplace, refrigerator, stove and picnic tables to seat about 70 people. Swimming is not officially condoned at the park but on a hot day it's tough to resist taking a dip.

Camping is popular at the park's 85 wooded camp-sites, but since the park is open on a first-come, first-served basis, plan on setting up early or arriving midweek during the busy summer months. Since electricity is available at all campsites, this park is especially popular among RV campers.

The beautiful view from the edge of the cliff and convenient public access to Green Bay waters combine to make this park a favorite.

Red River County Park (7 acres)
The Red River flows through this seven-acre Kewaunee County Park north of Dyckesville. The park provides access to Green Bay waters with a boat-launching facility. Picnic tables, grills, a shelter and privy are provided.

Chaudoir's Dock County Park (5 acres)
Located off Highway N, west of Namur, Chaudoir's Dock County Park offers two substantial docks serving as an emergency harbor of refuge for small boats. At times, the dock and nearby waters provide excellent fishing opportunities. The north dock was substantially improved in the fall of 1977 and is in excellent condition. The south dock is leased to a private party.

Haines Town Park (2.5 acres)
You won't find any facilities here, but who needs a picnic table when you've got a sand beach? Located on Riley's Bay, off County M, Haines Town Park is protected from the wind from all directions save west-northwest. Except for the beach, much of the area is wetland.

Tornado Memorial Park (2.6 acres)

This wayside park is located on Highway 57 about three miles northeast of Brussels. It was established to mark the location where 60 people lost their lives during the tragic Peshtigo fire of 1871. The park takes its name from the "tornado of fire" that leapt the waters of Green Bay to ignite the dry forests of southern Door County. A historical tablet pays tribute to a handful of pioneers who survived the inferno by taking refuge in the nearby well which remains standing.

Sugar Creek County Park (40 acres)

Recently upgraded, this county park off County Trunk N offers an excellent boat-launching ramp (fee) for fishermen seeking access to Green Bay. Those attempting to launch during poor weather should avoid this landing since the exposed bayshore is frequently buffeted by intense storms and the associated white-caps can be very intimidating. A large, wooded section of the park is entirely undeveloped and rustically appealing. Sugar Creek, for which the park is named, is popular with smelt dippers.

Gardner Town Park (1.5 acres)

There are no facilities at this unmarked park that fronts the waters of Little Sturgeon Bay. Waterfowl appreciate this area because it is very low and marshy.

Claflin Memorial County Park (.02 acre)

Called a county park, Claflin Memorial Park is more accurately a historical marker commemorating Increase Claflin, who in 1835 became the first permanent white settler in Door County. Located off County Hwy CC, the site is identified by a low rail fence along each of its 28-foot-long sides. A large elm tree and a stone monument are framed by the fence. A picnic table and grill accommodate the occasional picnicker. The Door County Historical Society has officially recognized this locale as a historical site.

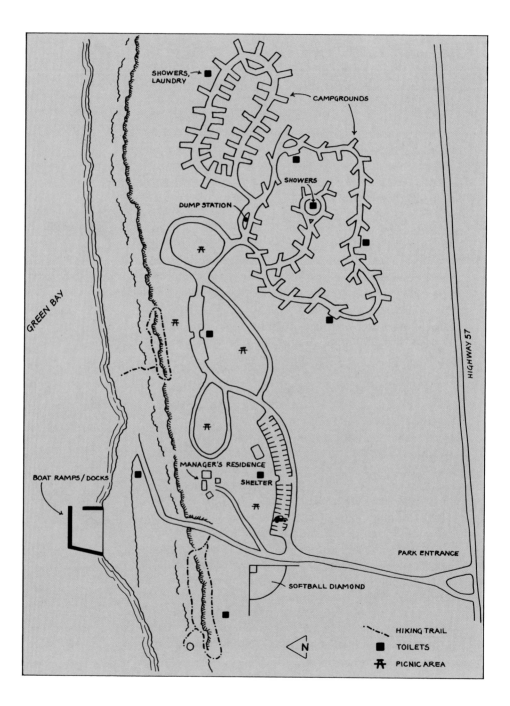

SHOWERS, LAUNDRY

CAMPGROUNDS

SHOWERS

DUMP STATION

GREEN BAY

HIGHWAY 57

BOAT RAMPS / DOCKS

MANAGER'S RESIDENCE

SHELTER

PARK ENTRANCE

SOFTBALL DIAMOND

N

HIKING TRAIL

TOILETS

PICNIC AREA

Idlewild Town Park (6.5 acres)

Much of this park is low-lying and marshy. Located near the waters of Sawyer Harbor, on County Trunk M, Idlewild Town Park offers views of Potawatomi State Park and provides a scenic landscape to motorists.

Forestville Dam County Park (79 acres)

Once a popular fishing and swimming area, the Forestville Pond, choked by weeds and filled with rough fish, today does not provide an enjoyable experience for either use. The pond was formed by damming a portion of the Ahnapee River during the late nineteenth century to provide power for a gristmill. The dam, an earthworks piled across the river, has been repaired and rebuilt many times over the years. Recently the dam's spillway was completely rebuilt. The pond does attract waterfowl and has traditionally been a popular hunting area. This park has parking for about 15 cars and provides access for canoeists heading down the quiet water of the Ahnapee River. It is also located near the Ahnapee State Trail and mountain bikers can gain access here.

VILLAGE OF FORESTS
The community of Forestville was named during its heyday as a lumbering village. When the timber cutting came to an end in the late 1880s, the stumps were cleared for farming. Today agriculture is the primary economy, although second-growth woodlots continue to dot the landscape.

Robert La Salle County Park (8 acres)

This eight-acre park is distinguished by a three-tiered landscape consisting of pebble-strewn Lake Michigan shore, then a level, grassy upland area and finally a higher, wooded plateau. Steep sandy bluffs separate each tier. A stairway provides access to the middle and top tiers. The Door County Historical Society has erected a monument here, commemorating this park as a landing site of French fur trader Robert La Salle. A small stream cuts through an interesting sandy ravine along the southern side of the park. This park provides plenty of parking room and offers one of the few public access opportunities to Lake Michigan along the southern Door shoreline.

(opposite page)

BAYSHORE
COUNTY PARK

Clay Banks Town Park (61 acres)
Over 3,000 feet of Lake Michigan shoreline comprise Clay Banks Town Park. This park is heavily wooded and boasts an excellent sand beach. You won't find any modern improvements to this park, but a road through this facility provides turnout parking opportunities for a few cars.

Sturgeon Bay Canal Town Park (20 acres)
Fishermen and naturalists share appreciation for this area. A breakwater pier offers a great view of the Canal Lighthouse (listed separately) built in 1899 and the operational Coast Guard station. Fishermen can cast their line into Lake Michigan from the pier in hopes of hooking a salmon or trout. Naturalists will enjoy trying to identify the plants tenuously anchored to the deep sand found here. The narrow one-lane road leading to this park limits its use, so plan to arrive early if you're hoping for a parking space. To reach this hidden jewel, exit Highway 57 at Sturgeon Bay on County U. Take U to Lake Road and turn left (east) to the mouth of the Sturgeon Bay shipping canal.

Portage Town Park (20 acres)
This historic town park has always been a hidden favorite of local beachcombers. It is located just north of the Sturgeon Bay Coast Guard station on Lake Forest Park Road. A small tablet marks the entrance and commemorates the location where Indians once portaged their canoes from Lake Michigan to Sturgeon Bay. The park's wonderful sand beach attracts swimmers and sea kayakers willing to brave the Lake Michigan chill. Surf casting for salmon and trout is a popular activity, especially in early spring.

CLAY BANKS
Red banks of clay rise nearly 100 feet from the Lake Michigan shore in the town of Clay Banks. Once a thriving trio of three villages, Clay Banks today is a single town dotted by farms and rustic lakeshore cottages.

PRESERVES

Gardner Swamp Wildlife Area

From Brussels, turn left (west) on County C. Follow C about three miles to Gravel Pit Road and turn right (north) into the area. Or, continue on C as it turns sharply right (east) to Pickeral Road. Turn right on Pickeral Road to Gardner Swamp.

FACILITIES:
   Day-use.

RECREATION:

   Hiking, bird-watching, hunting and snowmobiling.

Gardner Swamp Wildlife Area preserves 1,032 acres of swamp, hardwoods and white cedar forest sur-rounding Keyes Creek. It provides a refuge for water-fowl, white-tailed deer, wild turkeys and an occasional green heron.

Winter is a favorite time for backcountry explorers to strap on their skis and head into Gardner Swamp. The insects of summer are gone and frozen Keyes Creek provides an excellent thoroughfare through the marsh.

Wild turkeys were transplanted near here on the Brussels hill in the mid-1990s. Tracks in the winter snow provide evidence that Gardner Swamp is one of their strongholds. This is a popular spot for both white-tailed deer and waterfowl hunters so visitors may wish to avoid this area during Wisconsin's hunting seasons.

Located in the southwestern farm country of Door County, acquisition of land began in 1958. The need for this became apparent when beavers building dams on Keyes Creek continually flooded private land. During these periods it was noted that the beaver ponds held waterfowl, providing duck hunting opportunities. Thus, with the blessing of local landowners, state land ac-quisition was begun. Spring-fed Keyes Creek is the only stream in the Gardner area. This five-mile-long stream flows north through the swamp to Little Sturgeon Bay on Green Bay. Keyes Creek develops into an expansive marshland on the property, and cattail, bulrush and sedge are found in low-lying areas of the swamp.

BLOOMING DOORFODILS
Since the early 1900s, Door County residents have planted thousands of daffodil bulbs. The fruit of this labor blooms each spring when over one million daffodils greet the spring sunshine during the annual Door County Festival of Blossoms held in mid-May. Many of the daffodils in bloom include a special white and apricot colored variety known as the "Doorfodil." This unique variety has been cultivated exclusively for Door County.

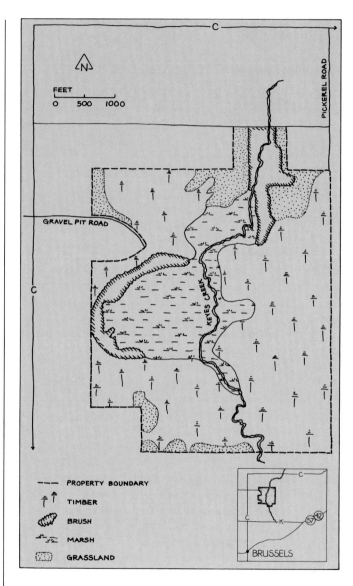

Gardner Swamp is an area of extreme importance to waterfowl on the Door Peninsula. Each year the area supports 30 to 40 broods of wood ducks, mallards and blue-winged teals. The area's close proximity to Green Bay and Lake Michigan also makes the swamp an attractive resting place for both migrating birds and visiting tourists in need of a rest break.

BEACHES

Haines Town Park Beach

A sliver of sand about 12 feet wide and a great view await visitors at Haines Town Park Beach. Located on Riley's Bay off Town Park Road, swimmers will find a shallow sand-bottom bay and a beautiful view of Snake Island in the distance. The beach is small but well protected from the winds on all sides except the west-northwest. A sign marks the park, and a small area is provided for parking. Excellent carry-in boat access is available.

Sand Bay Beach

Sand Bay Beach is an inviting, privately owned beach open to the public. This bay takes its name from the comfortable sand that cushions the feet of swimmers as they saunter in for a swim. The resort beach offers a concession stand where ice cream and other summer staples can be purchased. The water here warms quickly, making Sand Bay Beach one of the best spots on the peninsula for a June swim.

Portage Town Park Beach

The beach at Portage Town Park is lovely. This out-of-the-way Lake Michigan beach attracts few visitors, which adds to its appeal. The water is frequently chilly, but somehow that seems bearable when the waves are crashing and the sun is high. This is a historical site, marking the location where Indians and fur traders carried their canoes from Lake Michigan to Green Bay waters. Access is off Lake Forest Park Road just north of the Coast Guard station.

Forestville Dam Park Beach

The Forestville Pond provides swimming and sunning opportunities for bicyclists pedaling the Ahnapee Trail. It also provides canoes and kayaks and other small boats access to the Forestville Pond, an impoundment created by a dam that once powered a nineteenth-century gristmill. To access the park from the Village of Forestville go west on County J to Mill Road and turn right.

Sturgeon Bay Canal Park Beach

The city of Sturgeon Bay leases this beautiful 20-acre site from the Town of Sturgeon Bay for one dollar a year. You'll agree it's the best deal on the peninsula once you step onto the glorious beach that looks over the Coast Guard station at the mouth of Sturgeon Bay's shipping canal. A one-lane road leads to this beach, but parking is limited so plan to arrive early or pedal your bicycle to find a parking spot. To get to this hidden treasure, exit Highway 57 at County U in Sturgeon Bay. From U, turn left (east) on Lake Road and wind your way to the mouth of the shipping canal.

Sunset Park Beach

Sunset Park Beach offers swimming and the watchful eye of a lifeguard during specified times during the summer months, offering extra security for parents with small children. A bathhouse and restroom facilities make this a very popular "in-town" beach for visitors and locals alike. Access is off North Third Avenue (County B) from downtown Sturgeon Bay.

Fred J. Peterson Memorial Pool

A heated indoor public swimming pool named in honor of Sturgeon Bay shipbuilding magnate Fred J. Peterson is located near the shipyards on the city's east side. Showers and dressing rooms are available. Lifeguards keep an eye on the pool, which includes two diving boards. The pool is open seven days a week, including evenings.

Ottumba Park Beach

This Sturgeon Bay city park beach offers supervised swimming. Located near Potawatomi State Park, this beach offers excellent swimming opportunities lacking at Potawatomi. Restroom, playground, tennis courts and picnicking facilities are also available.

La Salle County Park Beach

La Salle County Park offers one of the few public access locations to take a swim in southern Door County. You'll have to make your way to the lower

STRAWBERRY CREEK

Strawberry Creek, which flows into Sturgeon Bay near the shipping canal, was the site of Wisconsin's first chinook salmon planting, in 1969. Today, a condominium project and private marina are located near the mouth of this shallow creek.

level of this three-tier park to reach the lakeshore. Here Lake Michigan either gently laps the shore or furiously charges the pebble beach, depending on its ever-changing condition. The park is named for explorer Robert La Salle, who landed here in 1679.

STATE TRAILS

The Ahnapee State Trail (15 miles)

The Ahnapee State Trail follows an abandoned rail bed between Algoma and Sturgeon Bay. To get to the trail-head at Sturgeon Bay, exit Highway 42-57 at County S south of the city. Take County S to Wilson Road. Turn left on Wilson Road and follow it to West Shiloh Road. The trailhead at Algoma is one mile north of Algoma on County M.

The Ahnapee Trail follows the Ahnapee River taking cyclists, hikers and horseback riders down an aban-doned railroad track through a cedar swamp, past two villages and along the dairy farm country of rural Door and Kewaunee counties. The trail is best enjoyed by mountain bike, as visitors spin through the woods and fields on an eight-foot-wide ribbon of crushed limestone.

Working in cooperation with the Wisconsin Department of Natural Resources, a group called Friends of the Ahnapee Trail has constructed a new bridge on the trail between Forestville and Algoma. They've also been instrumental in extending the trail from Algoma to the Village of Casco. Long-term plans call for the continued extensions of the Ahnapee trail to the city of Green Bay and beyond.

The Ahnapee was designated as a National Recreation Trail in 1976. It now forms a link in the 1,000-mile-long Ice Age National Scenic Trail, which begins at Potawatomi State Park. Bikers and hikers share the trail with horseback riders spring through fall. During winter the eight-foot-wide grade becomes a snowmobile trail maintained by local club members.

Today the Ahnapee Trail extends over 20 miles from Sturgeon Bay to Algoma and on to the village of Casco.

A connecting section of trail now allows bikers to proceed on to the city of Sturgeon Bay.

Camping is not available off the trail itself, but cyclists will find Potawatomi State Park an excellent and convenient spot to roll out a sleeping bag. A pair of private campgrounds are located at the Algoma entrance to the trail. Leashed dogs are allowed on the trail but hunting is prohibited. Restrooms are available at Algoma, Forestville, Maplewood and Sturgeon Bay.

AHNAPEE
STATE TRAIL
The trail now extends to the village of Casco, south and west of Algoma.

There is no fee to use the trail but visitors are encouraged to make donations at either the Algoma or Sturgeon Bay trailheads to offset maintenance and improvement costs.

For information or to join the Friends of the Ahnapee Trail write P.O. Box 167, Forestville, WI 54213 or call 920-487-3214.

The Ice Age Trail

The observation tower at Potawatomi State Park marks the eastern beginning of the Ice Age Trail. Here one can climb the 225-foot tower. The Door Peninsula, part of the Niagara Escarpment, split the advancing glacier into the Green Bay Lobe to the west and Lake Michigan Lobe to the right. Potawatomi State Park is situated on this limestone ridge, which extends from here to Niagara Falls. Winding along a 1,000-mile pathway, the Ice Age Trail follows the hills, ridges, lakes and marshes carved by this glacial ice. Beginning at Potawatomi, the trail heads through Kewaunee and Manitowoc counties before reaching its southern terminus between Milwaukee and Madison. Winding north through central Wisconsin, the trail cuts west through the Northern Highland–American Legion State Forest and then to Interstate Park on the banks of the St. Croix River. The trail within Potawatomi follows the Tower Trail to the Sturgeon Bay shoreline, then continues south along the shore before leaving the park at Shore Road. Ice Age National Scenic Trail symbols mark the route from the tower.

To date about 350 miles of the Ice Age Trail have been established in segments ranging from 2 to 40 miles in length. Development of this ambitious project began in the 1950s when Ray Zillmer of Milwaukee proposed a hiking trail that would follow the moraines marking the advance of the last glacier in Wisconsin. Volunteers began building the first segment of the trail, and in October of 1980 Congress designated the Ice Age Trail a National Scenic Trail, one of only eight in the country.

Today, a special Ice Age biking trail, sometimes coinciding with the Ice Age Trail and at times separate, stretches across Wisconsin. The Ahnapee Trail, just south of Potawatomi State Park, is one of these dual-use trails. The Ice Age Trail crosses both public and private land.

For more information on the Ice Age Trail contact: Ice Age Trail & Foundation, Inc., P.O. Box 423, Pewaukee WI 53072. Phone: 414-691-2776 or 800-227-0046. Web site: www.iceagetrail.org.

BICYCLE TOURS

Bayshore Breeze (12 miles)

This ride follows the Sturgeon Bay shoreline, then climbs a bluff northeast of the city before returning to the bayshore. This route shows off the developed area along the shore as well as country roads and cherry orchards just outside the city of Sturgeon Bay. A swimming beach is available at Sunset Park, where this tour begins.

Beginning at Sunset Park at the north end of Third Avenue in Sturgeon Bay, head up the shore on County B (North Third Avenue). You'll immediately pass Little Lake, which is noted for its resident duck and geese populations. Potawatomi State Park is visible across the bay, and sharp-eyed cyclists might even locate the Sherwood Point Lighthouse in the distance. After traveling four miles, turn right on Old County OR and begin climbing the bluff. Looking back you'll be rewarded with a great view of the waters of Sturgeon Bay. Bear left at the intersection of Martin Road one-quarter mile before turning right on Whitefish Bay Road. At the next stop sign turn right on County HH, making another climb up two small hills. On the crest of the bluff do not turn right but continue straight across Dunn Road until you reach the intersection of Walker Road and Peterson Road. Bear right on Peterson Road, descending down the bluff to Gordon Road. Turn right on Gordon Road and continue your descent across County HH and down to County Trunk B. Turn left and you'll find it's only a one-mile ride back to the beach at Sunset Park.

Ship Canal Clipper (13.5 miles)

This tour of the lakeshore crosses the portage trail that Indians once used to shuttle their canoes from Lake Michigan to Green Bay waters. You'll be traveling narrow, wooded lakeshore roads that provide access opportunities for swimming. Pack your swimsuit if

BAYSHORE
BREEZE
BICYCLE
TOUR

CAPE TOWNSEND
The Door Peninsula may have once been known as Cape Townsend. At least two maps dated between 1835 and 1841 bear the name Cape Townsend in reference to the Door Peninsula. The name honors Charles Townsend, an English politician who financed exploration of the Great Lakes. The Menominee Indian name for Door County was Kenatao, meaning "cape." The French voyageur term was La Porte des Morts meaning "door of the dead."

There are many popular spots throughout Door County to begin a bike ride.

you're brave enough to face the chilling waters of Lake Michigan.

Begin at the Sturgeon Bay Coast Guard station (follow the signs from Highways 42-57 at Sturgeon Bay). Turn right (north) leaving the Coast Guard station on Lake Forest Park Road. After one-quarter mile you'll reach a historical marker commemorating the portage trail. Portage Town Park is a great place to take a swim, but this is Lake Michigan so be prepared for a cool dip. Continue north on Lake Forest Park Road to County TT and turn right before making a quick left on North Lake Michigan Drive. This scenic, narrow road crosses County T where it becomes Brauer Road. Take Brauer Road to Forest Road and turn left. Continue past County View Road to Mathey Road and turn left on Mathey Road. Crossing County T again you'll see

54

evergreen plantings by a Sturgeon Bay commercial landscape nursery. White-tailed deer enjoy these tender young trees and it's a constant battle to discourage them from munching on this profitable crop. Following Mathey Road across County TT you'll pass the Door

**SHIP CANAL
CLIPPER
BICYCLE TOUR**

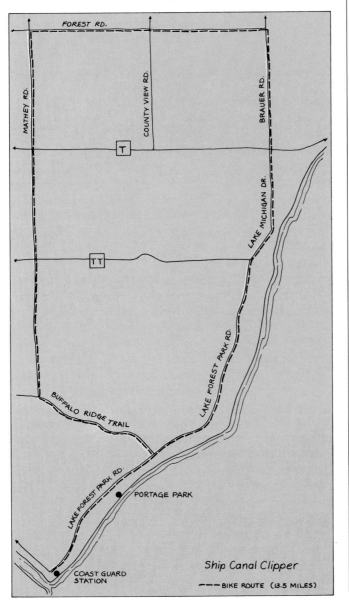

Ship Canal Clipper

- - - BIKE ROUTE (13.5 MILES)

County Rod and Gun Club before reaching Buffalo Ridge Trail. Turn right on this nicely wooded road and you'll pedal through a stand of birch, maple and evergreen trees. Passing Buffalo Ridge Road you'll reach Lake Forest Road. Turn right on Lake Forest Road and follow it past Portage Park and back to the Coast Guard station.

CANOE AND KAYAK ROUTES

Sawyer Harbor Swing
Summer and fall are the best times to explore Sawyer Harbor by canoe or sea kayak. The trip is best undertaken by those with an intermediate level of experience; it can take an hour or all day. Paddlers will find easy access, excellent fishing and interesting scenery despite development along Sawyer Harbor. Put in at the boat launch in Potawatomi State Park and either hug the Potawatomi park shoreline to the right (southeast) or head left (northwest) of the landing to explore the nooks and crannies of Sawyer Harbor while casting for northern pike, smallmouth bass or walleye along the shoreline. Homes and cottages line much of Sawyer Harbor's shoreline, but wooded wetland is also found, and the shoreline of Potawatomi is undeveloped. The two small islands in Sawyer Harbor are privately owned and trespassing is not allowed. Return to the boat landing and relax in the park before heading home.

Kayakers who take off around the harbor will enjoy the view of the Sherwood Point Lighthouse which rests on the limestone bluff which overlooks the entrance to Sturgeon Bay. Built in 1883, the lighthouse is no longer manned. The grounds are no longer open to the public but while pausing in your boat, it's an interesting place to ponder the lonely life of a lighthouse keeper. The navigation chart for the area is NOAA #14910.

Little Sturgeon Saunter
Keyes Creek finds an outlet at Little Sturgeon Bay and so do paddlers eager to put in a good workout. Exit Highway 57 west on County C at Brussels. Turn right on

County CC and follow it to its conclusion. Turn right to get to Little Sturgeon Bay. The natural harbor off Green Bay is well protected but it pays to keep your eyes on the weather. It takes about an hour to explore the scenic coves along the jagged shoreline. If you want to stay on the water longer, Little Sturgeon Bay is one of the most popular yellow perch fisheries on the peninsula.

Ahnapee River Adventure

The Ahnapee is a meandering quiet-water river with some development. The marshy shore and farm fields provide a quiet rural setting. To get to the put-in at Forestville Dam Park, exit Highway 57 south of Sturgeon Bay at Highway 42. Head south to Forestville, then right (west) on County J to Forestville Park. This 79-acre park offers ample parking, picnic tables and restrooms. The trip down the river takes a full day since a shuttle return is required.

The Ahnapee River follows the Ahnapee State Trail as it meanders through southern Door and northern Kewaunee counties. Paddlers are likely to startle water-fowl, and quiet observers may happen upon white-tailed deer along this route. The murky water is home to northern pike and a spring and fall run of steelhead trout. The take-out for this trip is at Olson Park near the intersection of Highway 42 and County S in Algoma. Ample parking is available. A bike shuttle is also possible via the Ahnapee State Trail if you feel secure leaving your bicycle locked at the put-in. Try this paddle in early fall.

Portage Park Paddle

Kayakers can put in at Portage Park immediately north of the Sturgeon Bay Coast Guard Station on Lake Forest Park Road on the Lake Michigan side of the peninsula. When the waters are calm beginners can handle this, and on stormy days kayakers wanting a little lakeshore whitewater will be pleased to find a rolling surf here as waves torment the beach. If it's quiet water you're in search of, head to the bay side of the peninsula.

The sandy beach provides a convenient put-in for a

flat water summer cruise as well. To your immediate right, the Coast Guard pier guards the ship canal. This man-made passage to Sturgeon Bay provides passage to Green Bay waters if you're up for a major cruise. Heading left (north) up the coast you'll pass a collection of summer homes; during autumn, residents can sometimes be found surf casting for steelhead trout.

CITIES, TOWNS AND VILLAGES

Sturgeon Bay (pop. 9,118)

Sturgeon Bay stands as gatekeeper to the northern Door Peninsula, requiring all who pass to admire the beautiful view this natural harbor presents from the two bridges that connect the two sides of the city.

The city takes its name from the ancient giant fish species that was once so prevalent in these waters that in winter, settlers would stack five-foot-long sturgeon on the dock like cords of wood. Few sturgeon now ply these waters, most having disappeared under the same stresses of modern life that also claimed the Indian settlements that fished here prior to the white man's arrival.

The rich modern history of Sturgeon Bay begins with Father Jacques Marquette, a Jesuit missionary who in 1673 was the first white man to record a visit to this bay. Using an Indian portage trail, Marquette spent two days shuttling his canoe and supplies one mile overland from Green Bay to Lake Michigan near where the present-day ship canal divides the city of Sturgeon Bay. Portage Town Park acknowledges this trail and its colorful past.

A county park south of here marks the historic site where seven years later four members of an ill-fated expedition survived the winter thanks to the aid of friendly Indians. Local history has it that the group was a remnant of Frenchman Robert La Salle's first (and disastrous) expedition that fled an Indian mutiny at Fort Crevecoeur near the headwaters of the Illinois River. Having landed their canoes, the party apparently

SHIPBUILDERS
The Sturgeon Bay shipping canal, completed in 1878 and linking the waters of Green Bay with Lake Michigan, paved the way for Door County's shipbuilding industry. In 1897 a commercial drydock was built at Sturgeon Bay, providing the foundation for the city's shipbuilding industry. Production increased dramatically during World War II. Today construction of luxury yachts is still a mainstay of the Sturgeon Bay economy.

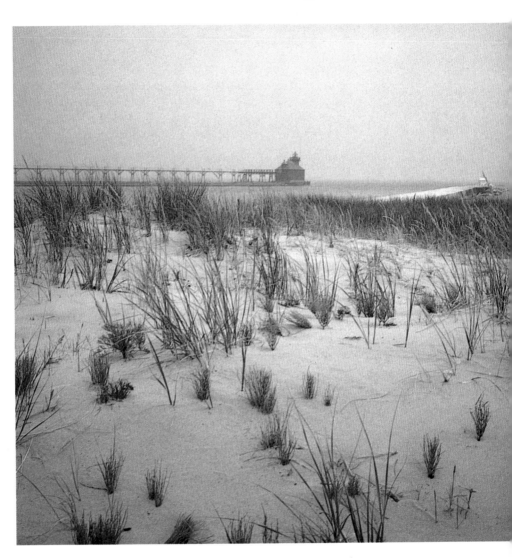

struggled over the Sturgeon Bay portage and paddled 14 miles up the bayshore to Egg Harbor. Weak and tired, the group sat out a five-day November sleet storm at Horseshoe Bay, consuming even their leather moccasins for nourishment. Void of supplies and low on hope, they returned to Sturgeon Bay where they had seen dry wood, "that they might die warm,"

Ancient sand dunes anchor rare plants at the mouth of Sturgeon Bay's ship canal.

SAWYER
NAMED AFTER
ITS POST OFFICE
The tiny village of
Bayview was platted in
the late 1870s, but
locals called it "Sawyer,"
after its post office. A
narrow strip of water
separated what was
then Sawyer from
Sturgeon Bay, creating
a communication and
commerce barrier
between the two
communities. In 1887
a private toll bridge
linked the communities
during the summer
months, while ice
provided a natural
bridge during winter.
In 1891, the two
communities established
a permanent link when
the state legislature
consolidated Sawyer as
the fourth ward of the
City of Sturgeon Bay.

according to expedition member Henri de Tonty. It was here that Onanquisse, a mighty Potawatomi Indian chief, showed mercy, offering the pitiful group food and shelter that ensured their survival.

Over 200 years later in 1878, the portage trail became obsolete when a ship canal, visible from the city's bypass-bridge, was blasted through the limestone rock, permanently uniting the waters of Lake Michigan and Green Bay at this point. Still in use today, the canal provides mariners a shortcut through the Door Peninsula and eliminates the treacherous journey through Death's Door Passage at the tip of the peninsula.

Soon after the canal opened, lighthouse keeper Rufus M. Wright lit the Sturgeon Bay Ship Canal North Pierhead Light marking the Lake Michigan entrance to the passage on May 15, 1882.

Nearby, the taller more powerful Sturgeon Bay Ship Canal lighthouse was constructed in 1899. The original 98-foot-tall tower proved unable to withstand the strong winds blowing off Lake Michigan and it was almost entirely reconstructed in 1903. Today, visitors have an opportunity to climb this lighthouse and bask in the panoramic view of Lake Michigan during the annual Door County Maritime Museum's Lighthouse tour held the third weekend in May.

Shipping played an important role in the economic history of Sturgeon Bay which was built on a foundation of logs and limestone. Thanks to its prime waterfront location, timber from nearby forests and limestone from nearby quarries played an important role in the city's development. The quarries surrounding the city of Sturgeon Bay produced a hard compact limestone which was shipped to ports throughout Lake Michigan for use in harbor construction while three sawmills buzzed with workers providing timber for a growing nation.

In 1858, Switzerland native Joseph Zettel acquired a farm about four miles north of Sturgeon Bay and established the first commercial orchard on the Door Peninsula. Zettel's high yields and quality fruit spurred the interest of professors at the University of Wisconsin, who concluded that the peninsula is remarkably well suited to fruit growing. Commercial production of red cherries began in 1896, and in 1922 the University of Wisconsin established a 120-acre fruit research station here.

The Door Peninsula continues to produce the third-largest cherry crop in the nation, cultivating the Montmorency variety of red tart cherries. Orchards here also produce 40% of Wisconsin's apple crop. Mid- to late May finds the fruit trees in bloom, and orchards of pink and white blossoms dot the landscape. Mid-July is cherry-picking time and visitors are welcome to pick their own cherries in many orchards. After the harvest, fruit stands cater to visitors, selling frozen cherries to use in your favorite recipes.

History buffs will enjoy Sturgeon Bay's downtown district. A tour map, available at the city's information booth, will guide you along the city's two districts listed in the National Register of Historic Places. You are welcome to walk, bike or drive the tour, which includes 100 buildings all dating back to the turn of the century or earlier.

Two museums of note in Sturgeon Bay recount the nautical and natural history of Door County. The splendid waterfront Door County Maritime Museum, located on the city's west side, opened in 1997. This museum replaces a seasonal facility which had operated for many years on the opposite side of the bay. Here visitors can trace the nautical history of Door County from the canoes paddled by native Americans to the 1,000-foot ore carriers built in local shipyards.

Across the bay, the Door County Museum traces the ethnic history of the county's farmers, fishermen and orchard growers. The Door County Museum is open May 1–October 31.

Sturgeon Bay remains the center of commerce, banking and industry on the Door Peninsula. Its boom-and-bust shipbuilding industry continues to be a source of employment, though the city is constantly expanding and diversifying its industrial base. Tourism remains an important industry, and major waterfront redevelopments on both sides of the bay are sure to increase interest in this picturesque city.

FISHING HOTLINE
Door County is well known for its world class fishing opportunities. The Door County Chamber of Commerce operates a 24-hour fishing hotline. To find out where the fish are biting, phone 920-743-7046.

Door County Library: 4th and Nebraska Sts. This is a full-service library with an interesting local history collection housed in the Laurie Room.

Miller Art Center: 4th and Nebraska Sts. This gallery is located in the Door County Library and boasts an excellent collection of paintings by Door County artists.

Door County Museum: 4th and Michigan Sts. This museum's emphasis is Door County's ethnic past, including the peninsula's Belgian, German and Scandinavian heritage. Admission fee. 920-743-5809

Door County Maritime Museum: 120 North Madison Ave. This 20,000 square foot waterfront museum recalls the long and varied nautical history of Door County. Open year around. Admission fee. 920-743-5958.

Sawyer Park Boat Launch Park: Located adjacent to the Door County Maritime Museum on the corner of Neenah and Maple Streets on the city's west side, this is a popular launching facility for excursions on either lake or bay. Picnic facilities available.

Ship Canal Park: Located on Canal Road, this park borders the U.S. Corps of Engineers shipping canal. Very scenic locale to watch boats chug to and from Lake Michigan. Access for shore fishermen to wet a line in the canal.

Lawrence Big Hill Park: Off 9th Ave. from Rhode Island St. The view makes this a great place for a picnic.

Garland Park: Off Business 57 across the bay. This two-acre, pleasantly wooded park is nice for an in-town picnic.

Martin Park: This park on S. 3rd Ave. has picnic tables and a band pavilion. It is also home to Peterson Memorial Pool where residents and visitors alike may enjoy swimming in this indoor year-round facility. It's named for shipyard entrepreneur Fred J. Peterson.

Farm Market: Fresh vegetables, local crafts and flowers are offered Saturdays from 8–noon, May–October at the corner of 4th Ave and Michigan Streets.

LAKE DEPTHS
The waters of Green Bay reach a maximum depth of a little more than 100 feet while Lake Michigan reaches a depth of more than 900 feet.

Little Lake Park: Off N. 3rd Ave. This borders Sunset Park and has a 24-acre lake stocked to provide fishing for children. Tame ducks live here, so be on the lookout as you drive in. Boat launching facilities provide access to Sturgeon Bay.

Bay View Park: Located next to the downtown bridge. This park has a nice sunset view of the bay from the west side of the city. Picnic facilities available.

Memorial Field: Off Michigan Ave. at 12th St. This lighted athletic field hosts major local sports events.

Sunset Park: N. 3rd Ave. A popular in-town swimming beach, tennis courts, playground equipment and picnic grounds are located here. A lifeguard is on duty at specified times.

Ottumba Park: On Juniper St. on the west side. There is an excellent swimming beach and a picnic ground here. A lifeguard is on duty at specified times.

Sturgeon Bay Canal Town Park: There's a beautiful little beach here southwest of the shipping canal. From Highway 57 exit at County U to Lake. Turn left (east) to the beach and the 20-acre park.

Portage Town Park: Just northeast of the Coast Guard Station off Lake Forest Park Road, this historic park has a nice small beach.

Door County Chamber of Commerce: Box 406, Sturgeon Bay, WI 54235 Phone 920-743-4456. Web site: www.doorcountyvacations.com. The office is located at the southern entrance to Sturgeon Bay on Highway 42-57.

Sturgeon Bay Information Center: Box 212, Sturgeon Bay, WI 54235. Phone: 920-743-6246. Open seasonally, the Sturgeon Bay area visitor center is located near the Door County Chamber of Commerce office at the entrance to Sturgeon Bay on Highway 42-57.

Robert La Salle County Park: Due east of Brussels on Lake Michigan. Access is off County U just south of County J. This 80-acre park offers a nice view of Lake Michigan as well as a pebble beach. There are facilities for picnicking.

LIGHTHOUSE TOURS

Each year, the Door County Maritime Museum hosts its annual Lighthouse Walk during the third weekend in May. During the walk visitors can get a first-hand look at Door County's historic maritime past. Something of a misnomer, the "walk" also includes narrated boat tours of Door County's Plum, Chambers and Pilot Island Lighthouses. To join the tour, call the Door County Maritime Musuem, phone 920-743-5958.

Forestville Dam County Park: Southeast of Brussels on the Ahnapee River. Take County J to the park, which is just past the intersection with County D. The park is adjacent to the Ahnapee State Trail and is a nice place for a picnic.

Chaudoir's Dock County Park: West of Brussels off County N. This 9-acre park offers a boat launch onto Green Bay and picnic facilities.

Haines Town Park: This 2.5-acre park is off Town Park Road north of County C at Riley's Bay. There is an unimproved small boat landing and a small beach.

Tornado Memorial Park: This is a wayside with picnic opportunities on Highway 57 north of Brussels.

Sugar Creek County Park: Access to this park is off County N on Green Bay. It's possible to launch small boats here. The park covers about 40 acres.

Gardner Swamp Wildlife Area: Six miles northeast of Brussels. Take County C to Gravel Pit Road. There are no marked hiking paths but public hunting is permitted in season for deer, ruffed grouse and waterfowl in this 1,032-acre preserve.

Brussels (pop. 1,159)

Amid the farms and fields of southern Door and bordering Kewaunee and Brown counties, visitors will find one of the largest rural Belgian settlements in America. A few of these folks still speak the native languages of their grandparents, either French or Walloon. Even when the residents speak English, visitors are likely to note a dialect unique to this part of Wisconsin.

The first Belgian immigrants carved their homes and farms from the forested wilderness surrounding the hamlet of Champion near the southern end of the peninsula. Letters to their relatives back home promising a land of timber and farm fields brought a wave of immigration in the mid-1800s.

Travelers will find evidence of this early settlement

when they visit the tiny, close-knit communities of Thiry Dames, Rosiere and Walhain. In 1989 the 3,500 acres surrounding these hamlets were placed on the National Register of Historic places. Known as the Namur Belgian-American Historic District, the area was upgraded in status to a National Historic Landmark in 1991, one of only 2,000 sites nationwide.

Of the 261 buildings included in the District, 41 are farmsteads with log cattle barns, summer kitchens or "bake ovens," wayside chapels, granaries, corn cribs and silos.

Preserving the historic barns, homes and outbuildings remains a constant struggle, according to University of Wisconsin professor William Tishler, a Door County native who laid much of the academic groundwork to attain the historical designation. He cautions against taking the landmarks for granted, saying, "We've got to fight to keep the good things we have from the past, in this area and throughout the whole peninsula."

The surprising number of red brick farmhouses that dot the highway, especially between Namur and Brussels, can be linked to the devastating Peshtigo Fire of 1871. During the fall of that year the logged-over bayshore woods was a tinderbox due to a hot, dry summer. As isolated fires burned in the cutover, smoke and ash rained down on Green Bay. Then, on October 8, one day prior to the Great Chicago Fire, strong winds fanned separate flames, creating an immense pillar of fire that was described as a "tornado of flames." Before the disaster was complete, 1,200 people had perished and whole villages were destroyed.

The Peshtigo Fire left in its wake about 5,000 homeless Belgian immigrants. It seemed their American dream had ended. But with help from their southern neighbors these hearty settlers rebuilt. They replaced their wood frame homes with brick structures that would be better able to withstand a second inferno, which, thankfully, has never arrived.

ROBINSONVILLE CHAPEL

The Belgian community of Champion marks the location where many contend the "Queen of the Heavens" appeared to a young farm girl named Adele Brice during the 1860s. Adele was instructed to "Gather the children of this wilderness and teach them what they need to know about salvation." This lovely and mysterious chapel is thought to be the site of many divine miracles. Today, the hall of the sacristy is filled with canes and crutches left by those cured of their afflictions. Hundreds gather from across the world each August to celebrate the Feast of the Assumption in a grand procession that winds through the church grounds.

A CELEBRATION OF HERITAGE

Brussels holds its annual Belgian Days Festival the second weekend in July. It's a great time to explore this area and enjoy some Belgian tripe (a Belgian sausage made from pork and cabbage) and Belgian pies.

BAYSHORE

ELLISON BAY MEN'S CLUB PARK
ELLISON BAY WOMEN'S CLUB PARK & BEACH
ELLISON BLUFF COUNTY PARK

SISTER BAY VILLAGE PARK & BEACH
GATEWAY VILLAGE PARK
SISTER BAY ATHLETIC FIELD
ANDERSON DOCK
EPHRAIM VILLAGE PLAYGROUND
NICOLET BAY BEACH
PENINSULA STATE PARK

CHAMBERS ISLAND LIGHTHOUSE TOWN PARK & BEACH

EPHRAIM PUBLIC BEACH
FISH CREEK TOWN PARK
FISH CREEK VILLAGE BEACH
SUNSET TOWN PARK
FISH CREEK COMMUNITY CENTER PARK

EGG HARBOR VILLAGE PARK & BEACH
HARBOR VIEW VILLAGE PARK

FULLER TRACT NATURAL AREA

FRANK E. MURPHY COUNTY PARK & BEACH

☒ STATE PARKS
● TOWN, VILLAGE & COUNTY PARKS
▲ PRESERVES
■ BEACHES

Through the Windshield

AN OVERVIEW OF THE BAYSHORE

Bayside beaches and waterfront campsites bring thousands of visitors each year to Door County's western shore. The reason they arrive is as varied as their backgrounds, but it seems all are seeking the serenity of a sunset or the comfort of a sandy beach.

The bayshore is considered by many the cultural center of Door County. Summer brings professional theater, music, dance, art, and education. The villages bustle with activity but those seeking peace and quiet can still find a quiet cove in which to relax.

To travel north from Sturgeon Bay, visitors can select either County Trunk B along the bayshore or State Highway 42. Both roads intersect at Egg Harbor but the scenic bayshore route rewards drivers and bicyclists with stunning views at the expense of slower travel. To travel this route, head north on 3rd Avenue (County B) from downtown Sturgeon Bay where you'll pass Sunset Park. This attractive city park has a lifeguard-patrolled sand beach on Sturgeon Bay, playground equipment, tennis courts and a boat-launching ramp. Be on the lookout for ducks crossing the road at adjacent Little Lake. Little Lake is a scenic pond with city parkland surrounding its shores. This lake is stocked with fish for the enjoyment of pint-sized anglers.

Continuing north 4½ miles from Sturgeon Bay, you'll find the remnants of an old limestone quarry which is now part of the Door County park system. This is an excellent spot to stretch your legs and examine the huge natural limestone foundation which supports Door County. Known as Quarry Park, the water surrounding this area is noted for its excellent smallmouth bass fishing. Anglers are often found wetting a line off the park dock in hopes of hooking a scrappy bass. The park also offers restrooms, a boat launch and picnic tables.

Stone quarrying was big business on the Door Peninsula in the 1800s. The immense limestone formations under the shallow soil coupled with its

(overleaf)

During the summer, Ephraim's historic Anderson Dock serves as a home to the Francis Hardy Art Gallery. The warehouse walls bear the art deco inscriptions of vessels that once lay anchor here.

proximity to Green Bay proved a bonanza to stone quarry operations like Leathem and Smith. Each spring, after the snow and ice had created new fissures in the limestone, the quarrying season would begin. In the early days four-man crews dislodged blocks of stone using 16-foot-long crowbars that weighed more than 300 pounds. A 12-hour day would net a man just $1.50.

Once loaded on barges, the rock was towed by a steam powered tug. Much of the stone wound up as rip-rap for the construction of piers, breakwaters and docks around the Great Lakes but it was also used to construct many buildings through the lakes-states region. By the early 1930s substitute building materials began to appear and the demand for stone began to crumble. Today little remains of the stone quarry industry except the walls of rock and remnant bay bottom boulders which shelter juvenile fish and terrify Great Lakes captains.

As you cruise up the bayshore, if you're longing for a swim or are anxious to get your kayak in the water, you'll be pleased to discover the next point of interest on your bayshore drive. Frank E. Murphy County Park (listed separately) has a great sand beach with excellent swimming opportunities. This park is very popular with local families and, after a refreshing dip, you'll under-stand why. The bluff opposite Murphy Park holds Tecumseh Cave, the longest cave in Wisconsin. The en-trance to this cave is private, however, and exploration is prohibited. From Murphy Park it's less than three miles to the Village of Egg Harbor. This once-sleepy community is experiencing rapid growth, but planners are taking care to maintain its unique charm.

Travelers departing Sturgeon Bay on Highway 42 will see farm fields and rural scenery as they head through the heartland of Door County. Unfortunately, zoning restrictions have not kept pace with lodging demands. Scattered developments are beginning to take their toll on the landscape. Sensitivity to this situation is on the rise, however, and unsightly developments are being met with increasing opposition.

Motoring over the Bayview bridge which bypasses downtown Sturgeon Bay, you can stretch your legs at

1998 TORNADO

In the summer of 1998, a tornado, which began as a waterspout over Green Bay, ripped through Murphy Park, uprooting all of the trees near the boat launch. The tornado then leapt the escarpment above the park before touching down again near Highway 42. Several homes and businesses were demolished but miraculously no one was injured.

RAM'S HEAD
ORCHID
SANCTUARY
Near Egg Harbor, nestled
below the steep bluffs of
the Niagara Escarpment,
a colony of delicate
Ram's head Lady's
Slipper orchids cling to
the rocky soil. So named
because its shape
suggests the head of a
horned ram, this is one
of only four locations in
Wisconsin where this
rare orchid thrives. The
Door County Land trust
has quietly been
acquiring land at the site
in hopes of establishing
a Ram's Head Orchid
Sanctuary to preserve
this native plant.

The Crossroads at Big Creek Historical and Environmental Preserve. Located on the east side of the highway, this preserve is a joint project between the Sturgeon Bay Education Foundation and the Door County Historical Society. Its goal is to foster appreciation for our natural and historical past through the use of an outdoor classroom. The preserve includes a short hiking trail around two wildlife ponds.

Pressing on, if you're interested in the agricultural past and future of Door County, you'll wish to pause at the University of Wisconsin Agriculture Experimental Station on Highway 42, just past the junction of State Highways 42 and 57. The Peninsular Experimental Station was established in 1922 when the University of Wisconsin purchased the John Kruzich Farm. This station is one of ten experimental stations maintained by the University. These units allow researchers to take their experiments from the laboratory to the field and make evaluations under the differing climate and soil types of Wisconsin. Even if the station is closed, you'll find an interesting state historical marker recalling the history of Door County orchards. The land just south of here became the first commercial orchard on the peninsula when Switzerland native Joseph Zettel began farming the land in 1858. The highway pulloff provides a convenient place to stretch your legs while reading the bronze tablet. If you're interested in a swim, exit Highway 42 at County G for a trip down the ledge to Frank E. Murphy County Park located on Horseshoe Bay before heading into Egg Harbor.

The Village of Egg Harbor is nestled in a protected harbor along the shore of Green Bay. A pair of village parks afford access to the harbor and pleasant views of this natural harbor. White Cliff Road follows the bayshore beside a striking cliff after which the road takes its name. This road parallels Highway 42 up to the small community of Juddville. Although most visitors travel Highway 42, White Cliff Road will not disappoint those seeking a colorful fall route when the leaves are brilliant and the air is crisp.

Sidetracking on County E, east of Egg Harbor, you'll encounter the Peninsula Center Sanctuary, also known as the Fuller Tract. A stone marker identifies the boundaries of this 160-acre preserve, which serves as a University of Wisconsin natural area. Continuing on County E, the road crosses a causeway dividing Kangaroo Lake before ending at Highway 57 just south of Baileys Harbor. Kangaroo is a 1,100-acre lake deriving its water from a spring-fed stream. The causeway separating the lake provides public fishing and boat-launching opportunities. A small public swimming beach can be found at the end of Beach Road on the western shore of the lake. (The water in Kangaroo is typically much warmer than either Green Bay or Lake Michigan.) A small boat launch is available at the end of O'Brien Road. Sand dunes separate the eastern shore of Kangaroo from Lake Michigan and add to its scenic value. Although Kangaroo Lake is dotted with cottages and resorts, its clear water and appealing wetlands make exploration by canoe or small sailboat most inviting.

Departing Egg Harbor on Highway 42 at Juddville, you'll encounter the access road to the Peninsula Players' "Theater in a Garden." This is the best nightspot on the peninsula as the sun sets over Hat Island on the horizon and playgoers are ushered to their seats. The all-weather pavilion allows the show to continue rain or shine and the affordable ticket prices bring visitors back year after year.

Descending the bluffside curve on Highway 42, you'll enter the lively community of Fish Creek, gateway to Peninsula State Park. The streets of this town bustle with activity from May through October. Rare is the summer weekend when their isn't some sort of festival happening in this hospitable village. During the off-season, however, the town slows down and many seasoned visitors time their vacations to take advantage of this relaxed pace.

At the intersection of Highway 42 and Main Street stands the stately and historic Noble House. Now home to the Gibralter Historical Museum, this building has stood vigil over the past century as autos replaced ox teams and powerboats replaced steamships.

A left turn at this intersection leads to Founders Square. Few of the original historic buildings in this

POW CAMPS
During the summer of 1945, a German prisoner-of-war camp was located in Fish Creek. Prisoners did construction jobs, wood cutting and cherry picking within Peninsula State Park and the surrounding area.

complex remain intact since a fire in 1984. Fortunately, a log cabin built by Asa Thorp and his brother in 1855 survived the fire. It remains the oldest structure in Fish Creek.

Just a short walk past Founders Square leads you through a wooded grove to Sunset Town Park on the western edge of town. Chambers Island is situated about five miles northwest of here in the shadow of the Strawberry Island Chain. Experienced sea kayakers could drop in a boat at this park and take a heading to this remote, privately owned island. Measuring one half mile wide by four miles long, Chamber's Island was named in 1816 in honor of Colonel Talbot Chambers, a soldier dispatched from Mackinac and appointed the task of establishing a military post here.

Today, the Town of Gibraltar maintains a forty-acre park located near the lighthouse on the northwest side of the island, and boaters frequently throw out an anchor to enjoy the inviting sand beach found here. A Catholic retreat house is located on the island, built on a sand isthmus separating the waters of Green Bay from inland Lake Mackaysee. This 354-acre lake is one of two inland lakes on Chambers Island.

Mackaysee, with a depth of 26 feet, is the deepest inland lake in Door County. It is an ancient glacial lake of striking natural beauty known for its bass, bluegill and northern pike fishing. There are a pair of islands in the lake, and very little development mars the scenic shore. About thirty acres of wetlands adjoin Lake Mackaysee. There is no public access to this scenic beauty.

The second inland lake on Chambers Island is little more than a four-acre pond known as Krause, Mud, or Lost Lake.

It's just a short walk from Sunset Park to Fish Creek Town Park located farther down the bayshore in the heart of the village. This cozy shore-front preserve overlooks Peninsula State Park, and serves as the center of activity during the many festivals the village hosts. The public dock here attracts skippers from throughout the Great Lakes and many captains begin their voyages to Chambers Island from this dockage. Small boaters and sea kayakers with Chambers Island

STONE FLEET
Barges were required to move millions of pounds of stone from Door County quarries to harbors throughout the Great Lakes. Lake schooners, steam freighters and even a number of elegant wood passenger ships became part of the "stone fleet." The engines, masts and sails were removed from these vessels and the hulls of these wooden ships were reinforced with iron and steel to support over one million pounds of stone.

72

as a destination should use caution, however, since beyond the protection of Strawberry Islands, lake swells can become threatening.

Back on the mainland, a short walk down Main Street will take you to the Fish Creek Village Beach. A marked swimming area and a sand bottom offer excellent swimming opportunities.

Just north of the beach, the creek for which the village is named is crossed by Highway 42. The creek originates in swampland and flows into Green Bay, forming the southwestern boundary of Peninsula State Park for a distance of about 1,000 feet. The stream is intermittent but at times a canoe can be paddled from Green Bay upstream.

The northern shore of this stream has been protected, as parkland, but unfortunately the southern shore did not receive similar protection and much of it has been lost to asphalt in recent years.

Continuing north just a few blocks you'll find the main entrance to Peninsula State Park. This 3,700-acre park is actually a spectacular peninsula on a peninsula, encompassing all of the bayshore property between Fish Creek and Ephraim. Established in 1910, the park protects seven glorious miles of Green Bay shoreline comprised of towering limestone bluffs, rich wetlands and second-growth northern forests. The park is a popular destination for campers, but reservations are mandatory during the heat of summer and the color of fall since all of the park's 469 campsites are reservable. A drive through this park is certainly worth the price of a one hour state park vehicle admission sticker if only to climb Eagle Tower or visit Eagle Bluff Lighthouse. The 75-foot-high tower, located near the Ephraim exit on shore road, rests on a limestone bluff perched high above the blue waters of Green Bay. Built by hand in the 1920s, Eagle Tower soars 200 feet above the Strawberry Island chain. The Strawberries, as they are called, consist of four small, privately owned islands: Adventure, Jack, Pirate, and Little Strawberry. The treacherous reefs surrounding this chain make development of the islands difficult, enhancing nesting opportunities for shorebirds. It was also these dangerous reefs which led to the 1868 construction of Eagle Bluff Lighthouse, located along Shore Road, within Peninsula State Park.

The historical society offers daily guided tours of the lighthouse from early June through mid-October. The small admission fee is used to fund operating and maintenance expenses.

Before leaving Peninsula State Park be sure to motor up Skyline Road for a visit to Sven's Bluff. This drive takes motorists over the park's highest terrain where you'll be rewarded with a commanding view along every curve. It is very common to see white-tailed deer along this route, especially near sunset. Parking is available at Sven's Bluff overlook which provides a constrasting yet equally inspiring view to that enjoyed from Eagle Tower. This bluff was once the site of a second observation tower until dry rot forced the removal of "Sven's Tower."

Departing the village of Fish Creek you'll be climbing a hill and making a sweeping curve past the Town of Gibraltar school grounds. The high school is home to the 750-seat Door Community Auditorium, where each August a three-week series of classical music concerts, called the Peninsula Music Festival, attracts both musicians and visitors from throughout the country. It was founded by the late Dr. Thor Johnson, conductor of the Cincinnati Symphony Orchestra.

Continuing on Highway 42, you'll find the southeastern border of Peninsula State Park providing a visual oasis as you travel from Fish Creek to Ephraim.

Reaching the northern entrance of Peninsula State Park, you'll encounter a championship-caliber 18-hole golf course complete with a pro shop and restaurant. A state park sticker is not required to park at the course but golf reservations are recommended and almost mandatory. They can be made by mail beginning in January for the upcoming season.

Winding into Ephraim you'll enjoy your first view of Eagle Harbor. This well-protected bay affords swimmers an excellent village beach when the wind is low and the sun is high. Windsurfers can frequently be seen skimming across the harbor when a breeze is blowing,

LIGHT-KEEPER SUPPLIES

Door County's Eagle Lighthouse keepers always looked forward to the arrival of the lighthouse tender laden with its annual supply of food, cleaning and repair items. Barrels of flour, sugar, cornmeal, salt pork, and corn beef were stored in the lighthouse basement. The keepers supplemented these staples with seasonal fruits and vegetables from the lighthouse garden along with domestic livestock and wild game.

and in late summer a concession offering parasail rides can send you soaring with the seagulls.

It is not by coincidence that most of the buildings in this picturesque village are white. An unwritten law requiring that buildings in the village be painted white or carry no paint at all has survived since Moravian pioneers staked their claim on this harbor in the nineteenth century.

Fishermen can frequently be found dangling nightcrawlers off the pier at Anderson Dock. This historic landmark was built in 1860 by Aslag Anderson. The exterior walls of this wooden building are painted with the various names of the boats that have anchored here over the years. This landmark now serves as a public art exhibit hall known as the Francis Hardy Art Gallery and is operated under the control of the Peninsula Arts Association. The Peninsula Arts Association was founded in 1937 to promote the arts in Door County.

Other historic sites in Ephraim include the Ephraim Moravian Church. (See a walking tour of Ephraim, listed separately.)

The development that has sprung up between Ephraim and Sister Bay in recent years has frustrated many long-time visitors to the Door Peninsula. The increased traffic and start-stop driving can take its toll on the nerves, and travelers wishing to avoid this congestion should plan to avoid this stretch during the peak season.

Sister Bay is the largest community in northern Door County. The village and its surrounding landscape are developing rapidly, but its downtown area maintains its traditional charm. A fine public beach and dock provide excellent access to Green Bay. The village and the bluffs that tower above it take their names from the two publicly owned "sister" islands offshore. These islands are preserved under the jurisdiction of the Wisconsin Natural Areas Preservation Council and provide nesting areas for shorebirds. Birds banded here have reportedly been recaptured from as far away as Panama. The twin "Sister Bluffs" rising above the village reach heights of 130 and 190 feet. Private developments top these bluffs, which provide an excellent view of Green Bay.

Settled in 1857, Sister Bay is best noted for its annual October Fall Fest. This is the largest community celebration in Door County, and thousands visit the village each October to enjoy the crisp autumn air and the colorful changing leaves. During summer, goats can be found grazing on the sod-covered roof of Al Johnson's Swedish Restaurant, creating quite a spectacle.

Departing Sister Bay en route to Ellison Bay, you'll be entering the northern orchard country of the peninsula. A trip east on County Z leads to Rowley's Bay and the mouth of the Mink River Estuary. This Nature Conservancy Preserve is best explored by kayak or canoe, although a walking trail is available off Newport Drive near Newport State Park. The Mink River is one of the most pristine natural areas of the peninsula. Alkaline springs feed this slow-moving river that flows through a vast wetland and past wooded shores before spilling into Lake Michigan at Rowley's Bay.

Continuing on Highway 42 you'll find a sidetrack to Ellison Bluff County Park leading to an impressive vantage point atop bluff headlands overlooking Green Bay. Access to the water is impossible because of the high limestone precipice separating the wooded parkland from the water. The scenic road leading into the preserve passes an old stone fence before turning to gravel through a cedar forest. An old logging road serves as a nature trail through this 88-acre park.

Proceeding on Highway 42 you'll reach the awesome bluff showcasing Ellison Bay. This bluff was once farmland, but pressure to exploit the outstanding view became intense and a resort now sits upon the overlook. Resort developers, however, took care to maintain the scenic approach, and motorists will not be disappointed as Ellison Bay unfolds before them.

Named for pioneer John Ellison, Ellison Bay was settled in the 1860s. Descending the hill you'll find the Ellison Bay Women's Park on the bayshore. A sand beach and picnic tables provide swimming and picnicking opportunities to the public. The Ellison Bay

FISH BOIL TRADITION

Fish boils have long been a part of the Scandinavian heritage in Door County. But the cooking of fish in kettles with potatoes and onions actually originated in lumber camps as an easy way of preparing the fish.

dock is home to many commercial and charter fishing operations.

Ellison Bay has become famous for popularizing the fish boil dinner, a tradition dating back to pioneer days. Fishermen and lumbermen settling the peninsula found an abundance of whitefish and trout in the surrounding waters. By adding potatoes and onions in a large pot, they created a simple and tasty one-kettle dinner. Today modern fish boils utilize basically the same recipe but add a few theatrics to interest spectators, including the "overboil." This is accomplished by adding a large amount of fuel to the outdoor fire just as the fish completes cooking. As flames shoot through the air the water boils over the large kettle, creating a spectacular sight. A cherry pie dessert completes the meal, reminding visitors that this peninsula is still considered "cherryland."

En route to the tip of the peninsula, travelers will enjoy turning left at Gus Klenke's garage on Garrett Bay on the outskirts of Ellison Bay. Gus Klenke is no longer alive, but his service station has become something of a local landmark. Comparisons to the fictitious town of Mayberry become apparent. Just two blocks from Highway 42 stands The Clearing. This private school for contemplation and study was founded by famed landscape architect Jens Jenson in 1935. Jenson developed The Clearing as a "school of the soil" in the belief that man must return to the soil and learn from nature if he is to find himself. Today the 120-acre grounds he nurtured maintains its enduring appeal. The Clearing is open weekend afternoons from mid-May through October.

A brief sidetrack off Garrett Bay Road leads to Door Bluff Headlands County Park. At over 150 acres, Door Bluff Headlands is the largest county park on the peninsula. The park preserves the woodlots surrounding 200-foot-high Door Bluff, but due to its rugged and challenging hikes it is rarely visited. Proceeding on Garrett Bay Road you'll drive along Hedgehog Harbor, so named because hedgehogs, commonly called porcupines, chewed through a boat left to winter on the shores of Green Bay by a pioneer fisherman. Winding along the shore into sleepy Gills Rock, you'll again join Highway 42.

If time is tight and you're anxious to catch the Washington Island car ferry, you'll be heading directly out of Ellison Bay on Highway 42. This road threads northeast past cherry and apple orchards to Gills Rock and on to Northport Pier. En route you'll pass the access road to Newport State Park.

Newport is a wilderness park preserving over 2,200 acres of undeveloped forest and shoreline. Its wonderful sand beach provides excellent swimming opportunities, and backpack camping is available. Just before you reach the state park on Newport Lane, you'll pass a wooden marker identifying the Schoenbrun Nature Conservancy. This one-mile-long trail provides walk-in access to the Mink River, a preserved freshwater estuary harboring endangered plants, wildlife and waterfowl.

Just before you make the final turn into Newport State Park, you'll encounter a gravel road leading to Europe Bay Town Park. This little park is sandwiched on both sides by Newport State Park and provides access to Europe Beach, perhaps the finest stretch of sand on the peninsula. If you're heading to the Northport Pier, you can continue down Timberline Road to join Highway 42 south of the dock or backtrack to the highway. Timberline Road is one of those quaint country roads that remind you why the Door Peninsula is such a special place.

DOOR COUNTY WINE

Winemaking in Door County began as early as 1862. Today the Door Peninsula Winery produces apple and cherry wine in a schoolhouse built in 1868 in Carlsville, north of Sturgeon Bay. The winery offers guided tours through fall.

STATE PARKS

Peninsula State Park

The entrance is in the village of Fish Creek off Highway 42, 25 miles north of Sturgeon Bay. Address: P.O. Box 218, Fish Creek, WI 54212. Phone: 920-868-3258

FACILITIES:

There are four campgrounds with a total of 469 family campsites, and three group campsites. All of these campsites are reservable by telephone. For up-to-date information or to receive a free state park visitor guide and campsite reservation application call 800-432-8747 or write: DNR Parks, Box 7921, Madison, WI 53707, e-mail: wiparks@dnr.state.wi.us. Additional information can also be found via the internet at the following address: www.dnr.state.wi.us/org/land/parks.

Private campground information may be obtained through the Door Country Chamber of Commerce; phone 920-743-4456. Reservations are mandatory during the summer, and recommended on autumn weekends.

The restrooms are modern and showers are available. A camping fee is charged; nonresidents pay more than Wisconsin residents. Also, the fees are higher during the months when the flush toilets are open. There is 30-amp electrical service available at 100 sites for an additional charge. The park is open year-round, but with reduced facilities in the off-season. A vehicle admission sticker is not required to drive through the preserve but if you park your vehicle you must have a one hour, daily or annual state park admission sticker. The park covers 3,775 glorious acres.

RECREATION:

The park offers hiking trails, a bicycle trail, mountain bike trails, tennis courts, a golf course, a swimming beach, ski trails, snowshoeing trails, canoeing and kayaking, an observation tower, a nature center with interpretive programs, an exercise course, a tobogganing

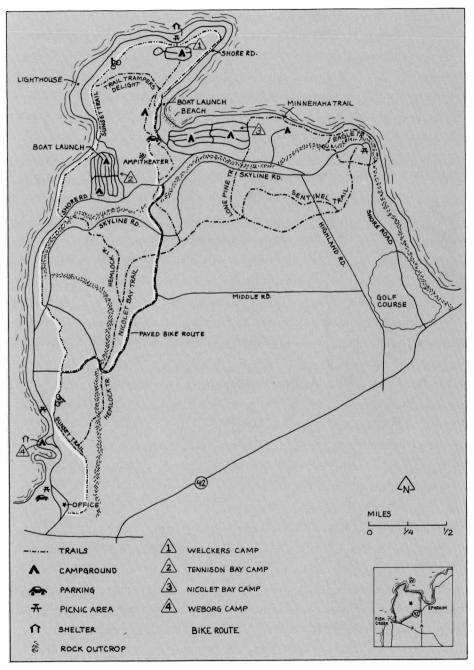

SHORE RD.

LIGHTHOUSE

TRAIL TRAMPERS DELIGHT

BOAT LAUNCH BEACH

MINNEHAHA TRAIL

BOAT LAUNCH

AMPITHEATER

SKYLINE RD.

LONE PINE TR.

EAGLE TR.

SENTINEL TRAIL

SHORE RD.

SHORE RD.

SKYLINE RD.

HEMLOCK TR.

NICOLET BAY TRAIL

HIGHLAND RD.

SHORE ROAD

MIDDLE RD.

GOLF COURSE

PAVED BIKE ROUTE

HEMLOCK TR.

SUNSET TRAIL

OFFICE

42

N

MILES

0 ¼ ½

─··─··─	TRAILS	
∧	CAMPGROUND	
🚗	PARKING	
🛆	PICNIC AREA	
⌂	SHELTER	
	ROCK OUTCROP	

1 WELCKERS CAMP
2 TENNISON BAY CAMP
3 NICOLET BAY CAMP
4 WEBORG CAMP

BIKE ROUTE

FISH CREEK

EPHRAIM

PENINSULA STATE PARK

slope, and two launch facilities for fishing and boating.

With its stunning sunsets, beautiful bays, craggy cliffs and towering trees, it's no wonder that Peninsula State Park is Door County's number-one attraction and the most popular state park in Wisconsin.

Peninsula State Park is located between Fish Creek and Ephraim about 70 miles north of Green Bay via Highways 57 and 42. A welcoming center greets visitors at the Fish Creek entrance. A vehicle admission sticker is required if you stop in the park even just to admire the view or climb the tower.

This is truly a four-season park. Summers in the park bring hordes of visitors escaping urban hustle and bustle. Many stake out a claim on the beach, some pedal through the park along roads that seem tailor-made for a country ride, and others paddle along the shore seeking solitude and seclusion.

Summer is also the season of education and entertainment in the park. Don't leave without taking in a performance by the American Folklore Theatre, presented from late June through Labor Day. These family-oriented musical productions feature a lively mixture of history and humor, well worth the small admission charge. You'll also want to consider the variety of programs conducted by the park naturalist. Rangers at the park are proud that Peninsula has a year-round naturalist on staff offering a variety of interpretive programs. These programs are aimed at increasing your knowledge of the natural world here with trees and cliffs forming the walls of your classroom.

A summer hike through the hemlocks will certainly renew your spirit, and a saunter through the pines will have you wishing you could bottle the aroma. Those with a bent toward exercise should not miss the Vita Course. This one-mile exercise circuit asks you to perform various tasks geared toward increasing your strength and improving your balance and coordination. It begins near Nicolet Beach.

An 18-hole golf course, considered by many the most scenic in mid-America, greets visitors at the park's Ephraim entrance. Getting a tee time can be difficult, so

WEBORG MARSH
Weborg Marsh is a ten-acre spring-fed marsh along Shore Road. This area has abundant aquatic vegetation.

reserve one by mail beginning in January, prior to your visit. Write: Peninsula Golf Associates, P.O. Box 275, Fish Creek, WI 54212. A tennis court is also in the park, but plan on arriving early if you wish to play.

Fishing is popular along the park shore where anglers search for coho, chinook salmon, rainbow, brown and lake trout, perch, bass and northern pike.

Paddlers will want to visit Horseshoe (Eagle) Island. This 38-acre island is visible from Nicolet Bay and provides hiking and picnicking opportunities.

Autumn travelers are greeted by a kaleidoscope of fall colors, and on October weekends the park can be just as busy as in mid-summer. Many find this time of year the best for hiking. The trails are never crowded, the temperature is brisk and animals are active, increasing your chances to spot wildlife. Winter finds a handful of hardy tent campers nestled in goose-down sleeping bags dreaming of hot spiced wine.

Cross-country skiers will find 19 miles of family-oriented ski trails geared to a wide variety of skill levels. If you enjoy snowshoeing, the park can accommodate you on two trails or you may break your own ground elsewhere in the park. The hill on the 17th fairway of the golf course has been set aside for tobogganing and sledding and remains off-limits to snowmobiles.

Bicycling is one of the park's most popular pastimes. The 5-mile-long Sunset Bike Trail makes up a section of the park's 9-mile designated bike route. This is one of the finest trails on the peninsula, offering everything Door County is famous for including water, woods and wildlife. Mountain bikers will enjoy bouncing down the park's cross-country ski trails which double as off-road routes during the summer and fall. A trail pass is required to access the park's mountain bike trails but no pass is required on the Sunset Bike Trail.

Hikers should lace up their boots or strap on their sneakers to gently tramp the park's 40 miles of trails. These trails wind below cliffs, cruise past sea caves and skirt wetlands. The trails also offer a chance to enjoy the park's vast array of wildflowers like Yellow Lady-slippers and the federally endangered Dwarf Lake Iris.

Wildlife lovers will be pleased to note Sandhill

PENINSULA PARK GOLF

Development of the park golf course began shortly after the park was established in 1910. It was begun by a group of Ephraim businessmen as a nine-hole course with sand "greens." Later the course expanded to its current 18 holes.

TOO MANY DEER?
Peninsula State Park is concerned the preserve may have too many white-tailed deer. Many species of wildflowers are no longer common as they once were. Trilliums are an example. It is suspected an overabundance of deer may be the culprit. To reduce the burgeoning deer population, portions of Peninsula State Park are open by special permit to hunters using black powder firearms during the regular Wisconsin deer hunting season in November.

CAMPING BARGAINS
Originally, camping was not limited to individual sites but to individual areas within the park. Camping was free at first and later a 50-cent-per-day or $5-per-year fee was charged.

cranes and wild turkeys have returned to the park where they find an oasis in which to raise their young and fill the air with the songs of spring.

The striking natural beauty of the park is largely the result of glaciers which swept through Wisconsin, then retreated, two million years ago. The last of these glaciers continued the work of earlier ice flows by scouring out the Green Bay and Lake Michigan basins leaving behind white cliffs, cobble beaches and blue water.

Modern visitors weren't the first to take an interest in this rich and inspiring landscape. Indian cultures, most recently the Menominee, Fox, Winnebago and Iroquois, roamed the woods of Peninsula State Park long before white settlements replaced their simple lifestyle. There is one known Indian encampment site within the park, but there is little doubt this area was heavily used by Native Americans.

It is widely suspected that Jean Nicolet, the first white man to visit the present state of Wisconsin, paid a visit to Nicolet Bay. This was to be a working vacation, however, since Nicolet had hopes of negotiating a treaty with Winnebago Indians. In the narrative of this journey, Nicolet says he stopped for a week at a place two days' journey from the Winnebago village. The principal Winnebago Indian village was at Red Banks, marked by a statue off Highway 57 north of Green Bay. Since it takes just two days to canoe from Red Banks to Nicolet Bay, it is indeed possible that Jean Nicolet was the first tourist on the peninsula.

Today little remains of this Native American presence. A totem pole on the park golf course, however, does mark the grave of Potawatomi Chief Simon Onanquisse Kahquados. Chief Kahquados was laid to rest here on May 30, 1931, before a crowd of some 10,000 spectators, a testimony to his popularity. Admired by both Indians and white people alike, Chief Kahquados was the last of a long line of Potawatomi chiefs who for centuries ruled over the woods, wetlands and wildlife of the Door Peninsula.

In 1842, Increase Claflin was the first white settler to homestead in what was to become Peninsula State

Park. In the early 1850s, Evan Nelson and Peter Weborg led some 35 families in settling a stretch of shore now called Weborg Point. Finding the soil poor for farming, these settlers soon turned to the surrounding waters where abundant whitefish and herring populations fed their families. As fishing began to decline, these

NICOLET BAY
CAMPGROUND

LIGHTHOUSE PAY
Early lighthouse
keepers at Eagle
Lighthouse received
a salary of $50 per
month plus supplies.
This was considered
an excellent wage in
the 1880s.

pioneers turned their efforts to lumber production, depending on the market created by steamships plying Green Bay waters. Eagle Lighthouse, established in 1868, helped guide these ships safely to dock at Eagle (Horseshoe) Island where they could take on firewood. By the early 1900s, steamships were making weekly visits to Fish Creek and Ephraim. But the forests were not limitless, and hopes to establish an agricultural base were not abandoned. In 1866, the first cherry and apple orchards were established on the peninsula. The cool, damp influence of Lake Michigan proved to be ideal for the growth of these trees, and fruit production remains an important aspect of the local economy. Today, a tribute to Door County's first farmer, Ole Olson, can be found in the Nicolet Bay Campground. Campers driving a tent stake through this shallow soil may suspect Ole died a hungry man.

Modern development of Peninsula State Park began in 1909 under the ambitious vision of its first superintendent, A. E. Doolittle. To supplement a limited operating budget, Doolittle raised money by leasing summer visitors the homes, sheds and barns which the state had acquired for the park. Camp areas, as opposed to campsites, were designated where campers could pitch a tent for free until a 50 cent per week or $5.00 per season rate was implemented.

As camping in the park became popular, semi-permanent shelters or "shanties" began to spring up around Nicolet Bay, then known as "Shanty" Bay. These "vacation" homes attracted many families including women and children who would spend the entire summer in the park while their husbands went to work, returning to the campground on weekends. This arrangement proved so popular that local merchants were soon delivering groceries to the growing park population.

Summer was also the season of "old time minstrel shows" within park boundaries. These shows were events with an estimated 1500 people attending a 1934 performance commemorating the addition of a permanent outdoor stage at Weborg Point.

Today this tradition of family entertainment

continues with summer performances by the American Folklore Theatre. For over 25 years this group of minstrels have combined music and story-telling under starry skies of the peninsula at an outdoor stage near the Nicolet Campground. A vehicle park sticker is not required to attend the performances which begin in late June and run through August.

Superintendent Doolittle is also credited with engineering the road system that sightseers and bicyclists find so appealing today. Convinced that scenic overlooks and "fire" towers would attract tourists, Doolittle supervised the construction of Eagle Tower and Sven's Tower within park boundaries. Once again, Doolittle's intuition proved correct and while Sven's Tower no longer stands, climbing Eagle Tower remains a "must-do" activity on any visitor's list.

Once the observation towers were complete, Doolittle turned his energy to the construction of two golf courses. With the help of Ephraim businessmen, Doolittle established a nine hole course with sand "greens" in the 1920s. In the 1930s the sand greens were converted to grass and the number of holes was brought up to 18.

The current championship course which challenges golfers was layed out in the 1960s by Edward Lawrence Packard, then an Ephraim summer resident. When completed it looked much as it does today, measuring 6,200 yards from the men's tees. The course's famous eighth hole was added in 1926. When consideration was given to changing this par three, 65-yard over-the-cliff hole, there was such an outcry that the idea was quickly dropped. Today white-tailed deer share the park course with golfers who enjoy sweeping water views and tree-lined fairways. Considered by many the most scenic golf course in mid-America, it is operated by a nonprofit organization called Peninsula Golf Associates. Those hoping to tee up in July are advised to send in their reservations in January. Write: Peninsula Golf Associates., Inc., P.O. Box 275, Fish Creek, WI 54212.

Until 1948, a girls' camp called Meenahga was operated within park boundaries. During its 32-year history, girls from the camp paddled canoes, took horseback riding lessons and even went skinny dipping beneath the moonlight in the waters of Green Bay. The operators of the camp hailed from St. Louis as did many of the campers. It's clear from their memoirs that Peninsula State Park and Meenahga was a special place to the girls lucky enough to pitch a tent here.

Camp Meenahga may be gone, but if car camping suits your style, you've come to the right place. Peninsula State Park offers the most complete public camping facilities in Door County. The park has four campgrounds: Nicolet Bay, Welcker's, Tennison Bay and Weborg. There are a total of 469 campsites, 100 with electricity. The campsites range from outstanding to adequate, depending on the location. Several sites are located directly on the water, and demand for these sites, particularly in Nicolet Bay, always exceeds the number available. Make camping reservations early to avoid disappointment.

If you arrive at Peninsula State Park on one of the many summer days when the "no vacancy" sign is posted, the park staff will attempt to accommodate you by suggesting private campgrounds in the area which typically have campsites available.

Nicolet Bay Campground

Nicolet Bay is the largest and often the busiest of the park's four campgrounds. Situated on Nicolet Bay, this campground offers waterfront campsites, easy access to the beach and glowing sunsets. The campground is divided into two sections, separated by the Nicolet Bay Beach and Day Use Area. The northern section of the campground has 44 sites while the southern portion has 144 units. Much of the campground is nicely wooded, except for the southeast one-quarter which is open field.

This campground, like the others at Peninsula State Park, has modern showers and facilities. Showers are also available at the Nicolet Bay Beach. This campground is open from Memorial Day weekend through mid-October, although not all campsites are available during May, September and October. The waterfront campsites on Nicolet Bay are in very high demand. Consider yourself lucky if you secure one, then sit back and enjoy the view—it's one of the best on the peninsula.

GAME FARM
During the 1920s and 1930s, Peninsula State Park was the location of the state's first game farm. The farm and rearing pens were located near the present group camping area and the open area of Nicolet Bay Campground.

CCC CONSTRUCTION
During the depression years, a Civilian Conservation Corps camp was established at the park. CCC men built towers, stone fences, hiking trails and many of the stone buildings found in the park today.

Tennison Bay Campground

Tennison Bay is an appealing family oriented campground with 189 sites. A new shower facility will surely add to its popularity and alleviate the waiting campers had to endure previously. It is the only campground in the park that is open year-round with winter water supplies. The campground has both shaded and open campsites, with those located in the spruce plantation particularly desirable. Boaters enjoy camping here because one of two boat ramps is located in the campground. A play area greets children eager to burn some calories after a long car ride. All campsites in Tennison Bay are reservable from May through October. The nature center, amphitheater and Nicolet Bay Beach are all a leisurely stroll away.

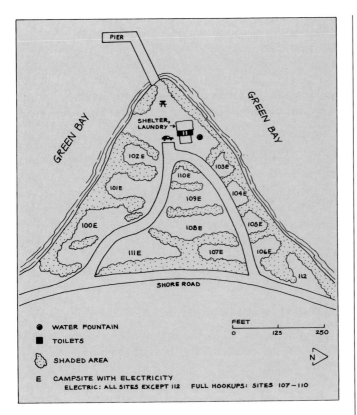

WEBORG
CAMPGROUND

CEDAR-SPRUCE
SWAMP
A cedar-spruce swamp is one of the two scientific areas within the park. This 53-acre forest contains a white cedar-spruce forest on an abandoned ancient Lake Michigan beach. Also present is a population of dwarf lake iris, a threatened species in Wisconsin.

Welcker's Campground

Welcker's Point is the site of an 81-unit campground noted for its heavily wooded campsites. There are six sites with electric hookups in the campground. New showers have replaced the outdated facilities which once marked this campground. Campers pitching their tents here have easy access to the Sunset Bicycle Trail, and it's only a short ride to the park beach. A shelter building adjacent to the campground on the bayshore provides a dry haven for campers caught in a sudden downpour. Wildlife in the park is abundant and there is an excellent chance of spotting white-tailed deer right outside of this campground. Welcker's is open Memorial Day weekend, then mid-June through mid-October. All campsites are reservable.

Weborg Campground

Weborg Campground has only 12 campsites. Even though many of the sites are unshaded, the campground is extremely popular because of its unique location. The waters of Green Bay border this triangular-shaped campground on two sides. All of the sites here have electricity.

A major attraction for those either staying here or visiting from other campgrounds in the park is the large concrete dock adjacent to the campground. The dock provides fishing opportunities and a scenic view of Fish Creek just across the bay. There are no shower facilities but this campground is popular with self-contained recreational vehicles. Weborg is open from mid-May through mid-October. All sites are reservable.

HIKING TRAILS

The Vita Course: This one-mile exercise circuit begins across from Nicolet Bay Beach near the overflow parking area. Eleven exercise stations instruct the user to perform various exercises designed to promote strength, stamina and coordination. Participants can walk or jog the course, pausing at each wooden station for exercise instructions. This is a great way to escape Nicolet Bay Beach for a quick romp through the forest.

Eagle Trail: The steep and rocky Eagle Trail (2 miles) traverses some of the highest bluffs on the Door Peninsula. It also skirts the base of these tall cliffs along a cobblestone beach while providing views of sea caves. The caves were carved thousands of years ago when previous lake levels were much higher. Budget 1.5 hours for this hike and pick up the trailhead at either Eagle Panorama, just west of Eagle Tower on Shore Road, or at Eagle Tower. Several springs, including Eagle Spring, can be found on this awe-inspiring hike but be advised conditions on this trail are sometimes wet and rough.

Hemlock Trail: A wonderful aroma drifts through the air as hikers saunter through the cedars on the 1.8-mile

Hemlock Trail. This trail provides access to the White Cedar Forest Natural Area, which is home to the federally threatened dwarf lake iris. Sharp-eyed hikers may spot this wildflower and others as the trail winds through stands of spruce, cedar and hemlock along a wetland. Be prepared to return via the same route, or pick up the Sunset Bike Trail for an alternate return on this one- to two-hour hike. The trailhead can be reached off Shore Road just south of Tennison Bay Campground.

Lone Pine Trail: Beginning at the southeast corner of Nicolet Bay Campground, the Lone Pine Trail climbs the limestone bluff that forms the backbone of Peninsula State Park. It then winds through a hardwood forest, passing the remains of the solitary white pine tree the trail is named for. Hikers have the option of returning to camp or continuing down the Sentinel or Nicolet Bay trails to form a loop back to the Nicolet Bay Campground.

Minihaha Trail: This short trail (.7 miles) along the lakeshore connects the Nicolet Bay Campground with the Eagle Trail. Pick up the trail near Nicolet Bay Campground site number 844.

Sentinel Trail: The popular Sentinel Trail loop (two miles) begins at Eagle Tower and winds through a maple, beech and red pine forest in some of the remote sections of the park. A .6 mile section of the trail has been graded to accommodate visitors who are physically disabled. Quiet hikers may see deer in the meadows on this hike. Budget one hour since the terrain is gentle, and pick up the half-mile connecting trail that leads to the Lone Pine and Nicolet Bay trails if you're up for more exercise.

Trail Trampers Delight: The short Trail Trampers Delight (.75 miles) traces its name to the early 1920s, when hikers walked from Nicolet Bay to Eagle Lighthouse. The heavily wooded trail provided escape from the summer sun, which made it a trail tramper's "delight." The trailhead can be picked up at the historic Eagle Lighthouse off Shore Road. The trail ends at Nicolet Bay Campground.

BIRD WATCHING
Over 125 species of birds live in or migrate through Peninsula State Park. The best birding spots are along forest-field borders, marsh-forest edges and along densely wooded lakeshores. It's best to wear drab-brown or green-colored clothing and carry binoculars and a good field guide.

Nicolet Bay Trail: The Nicolet Bay Trail provides campers at Welcker's Campround access to Nicolet Bay Beach as it winds past the overflow parking lot across from Nicolet Bay. This 2.2-mile-long trail then passes through stands of pine and cedar before connection with the Hemlock Trail to the south. The overflow parking lot across from the beach is a convenient place to pick up this trail if you're not camping at Welcker's.

Skyline Trail: The parking area off Shore Road just north of Mengleberg Lane is the trailhead for this three-mile loop to Sven's Bluff and back. The trail climbs through hardwood forests and meadows before ending at a wonderful overlook. Be sure to watch the signs carefully on the return trip, since this trail intersects with several others.

Hidden Bluff: The Hidden Bluff Trail is a three-quarter-mile spur loop off the Sunset Bicycle Trail providing easy access to the White Cedar Nature Center. Since adding the spur, park rangers are happy to report visitation at the Nature Center has doubled.

White Cedar Nature Trail: This one-half-mile, self-guided loop trail begins and ends at the White Cedar Nature Trail. Stations along the route interpret the ecology of one of the white-tailed deer which are often found feeding near the Nature Center at sunset.

(opposite page)

Lake-effect snow and groomed ski trails combine to offer outstanding cross-country skiing on the county's lakeshore.

CROSS-COUNTRY SKI TRAILS

Peninsula State Park reminds one of a postcard of Norway when five inches of fresh powder are weighing down the limbs of lofty pine trees along the cross-country ski trails. Breath-taking views, deep forests and snow-covered meadows beckon skiers to explore this picturesque winter playground. The variety of the ski trails is what keeps people coming back. The most challenging cross-country hills on the peninsula are found on the purple loop, while beginners will find both the white and yellow trails mellow and scenic.

You'll generally find snow here from January through March, but a phone call (920-868-3258) can give you up-to-date conditions. A Wisconsin state park admission sticker is required to park in the ski lots and winter camping is available for the (very) warm-blooded.

MILES
0   1/4   1/2

NICOLET BAY

LIGHTHOUSE

ANGLER PARKING

ANGLER PARKING

SHORE RD.

SKYLINE RD.

EAGLE TOWER

EAGLE HARBOR

SLEDDING

MIDDLE RD.

PURPLE

BROWN

BLUE

GREEN

YELLOW

RED

ORANGE

WHITE

BLACK

OFFICE

42

TRAIL DIFFICULTY: G = GENTLE
                R = ROLLING
                H = HILLY

(G)	WHITE LOOP	1.5 MILES
(R)	BLACK LOOP	3.0 MILES
(R)	BROWN LOOP	3.5 MILES
(H)	PURPLE LOOP	6.0 MILES
(G)	YELLOW LOOP	1.0 MILES
(R)	ORANGE LOOP	3.0 MILES
(H)	RED LOOP	3.5 MILES
(H)	GREEN LOOP	6.0 MILES
(H)	BLUE LOOP	7.0 MILES

············· SNOWMOBILE TRAIL

—·—·— SKI TRAIL

·+·+#·+· STEEP CLIMB

///// STEEP DOWN-HILL

------- SNOWSHOE / HIKING TRAIL

⌂ SHELTER

Park rangers groom 19 miles of ski trails, and most of these are one-way except short portions of the red, orange, and blue loops as indicated on the map. Skiers have four parking lots from which to begin their trips. Lots 1, 2 and 3 are accessible from the park's Fish Creek entrance while lot 5 is located off Highway 42 north of Fish Creek on County A. Lot 3, reached off Shore Road, caters to those wishing to ski the advanced purple loop. Warming shelters at parking lots 2 and 4 are open winter weekends. Plan carefully and keep an eye on the "you are here" signs which mark trail intersections. The mileage listed is measured from either lots 1 or 5, the two most popular winter trailheads.

The one-mile **yellow trail** is the park's easiest loop. Beginners will find a forgiving double-tracked trail traversing very gentle terrain through hardwood forests and old fields. Access from lot 5.

The **white trail** is another beginner's trail that's just a touch more difficult (1-5 miles) than the yellow trail. Access from lot 1.

Skiers with some experience will enjoy cruising down several challenging hills on the three-mile **orange trail**. There's nothing here too difficult for the intermediate skier. Perhaps that's why this is the park's most popular ski trail. Access from lot 5.

The **black trail**, also three miles, is geared toward the intermediate skier as well. This loop takes skiers through relatively remote areas of the park over gently rolling terrain. Expect a tough uphill climb where the black and brown trails separate from the white loop. Watch out for the steep curving hill on the last half-mile section. Access from lot 1.

The 3.5-mile intermediate **brown trail** shares the steep uphill climb encountered on the black loop where these trails separate from the white trail. There is a challenging downhill stretch where the trail merges with the purple loop. Access lot 1.

The **green trail** is a beautiful loop for an inter-mediate skier willing to travel six miles. Skiers venture through remote areas of the park, encountering a variety of forest and field. You'll find challenging hills between Highland and Middle roads. Access lot 5.

(opposite page)
PENINSULA
WINTER TRAILS

EAGLE
LIGHTHOUSE
Eagle Lighthouse was established in 1868. Today, the light is automated. Tours are conducted during the summer months by the Door County Historical Society, whose members have restored the structure to its 1890s condition. An admission fee is charged.

Fast downhills and plenty of climbing characterize a half mile of the red loop, but the other three miles are relatively flat. Access lot 5.

The **blue loop** is a great trail. The seven miles hit all the hills on the red and green loops plus a long section of lesser used trail. There's access to the purple loop if you still have calories to burn. Access from lot 5.

The exhilarating, challenging **purple trail** (6 miles) is groomed to accommodate both skate skiers and traditional striders. This is a popular training loop for ski racers. Hills are abundant and not for the faint of heart. Sven's Panorama is a "must see." This loop is not recommended for inexperienced skiers. Those wishing to hit the hills quickly have direct access for skate skiers available from parking lot 3.

SNOWSHOE TRAILS

Peninsula State Park has two "designated" snowshoe trails but those seeking solitude are welcome to break their own trail anywhere in the park.

The **Minihaha Trail** begins at Nicolet Bay where winter anglers park to access the ice of Green Bay. This trail skirts the shore of Green Bay on a gentle grade through the Nicolet Bay Campground and on to a secluded section of winter bayshore beneath the cliffs and sea caves of Eagle Bluff.

Sentinel Trail begins at Eagle Tower near the Ephraim entrance to the park. This trail takes snow-shoers through a peaceful and remote section of the park where adventuresome travelers can venture off the trail to make their own winter discoveries.

SLEDDING AND TUBING

For years the steep hill on the number 17 fairway of Peninsula's golf course has provided thrills and spills for families making a winter pilgrimage to Door County. You'll need a state park vehicle admission sticker to park your car here but the view from the hill-top alone is worth the price of admission.

HISTORIC CEMETERIES
There are many historic cemetery sites in Door County. Blossomberg Cemetery in Peninsula State Park is one such location.

TOWN, VILLAGE AND COUNTY PARKS

Frank E. Murphy County Park (14 acres)

Located off County B just south of Egg Harbor you'll find an excellent sand beach, a concrete fishing pier and boat-launching facilities to access Horseshoe Bay. This popular county park is named after Frank E. Murphy, a wealthy Green Bay businessman and prominent civic leader.

Across from the park is Horseshoe Bay Farms. Built in 1917, no expense was spared to construct the handsome barns located at the intersection of County B and G. These barns once housed Murphy's nationally famous black-and-white Holstein herd.

Murphy is the most popular county park in the Door County Park system. Still, the beach is rarely crowded and the dock is seldom busy. Recent improvements to the pier have provided excellent fishing opportunities for anglers, and expanded boat-launching facilities have made this a popular access point for boaters. A volleyball court, playground and picnic tables make this an excellent site for a family picnic.

HORSESHOE BAY FARMS
The Horseshoe Bay barns located across from Frank E. Murphy County Park were built in 1917. Some historians believe they mark the end of the pioneer building era in Door County since they were constructed using relatively modern techniques.

Harbor View Village Park (3.7 acres)

This small landscaped park in the Village of Egg Harbor has a few benches and a flagpole. It provides a scenic view of the Harbor and the village dock from Highway 42.

Egg Harbor Village Park (1.75 acres)

The Egg Harbor Village Park marks the center of shoreside activity in this picturesque community. The village dock provides 43 boat slips, but all but four are rented on a seasonal basis. There is a two-lane boat-launching ramp, and ample parking for both cars and trailers. Picnic tables and grills provide picnicking opportunities, and this is a great place to begin a bayshore bike ride.

Egg Harbor Nature Area (10 acres)

Located across from the Egg Harbor Village Beach, on County Trunk G, this relatively recent addition to the village park system adds a pleasant touch of green-space in the village center. Considering the park's relatively small 10-acre size, this wooded site harbors a rich variety of natural features including bedrock outcroppings, old glacial sand ridges and even a wetland.

Fish Creek Community Center Park (1.5 acres)

The Fish Creek Community Center on Highway 42 houses the Town of Gibraltar library and serves as a meeting place for local government. There are a pair of tennis courts next to the library, but parking is limited, so you may wish to secure a parking place on Highway 42.

Sunset Town Park (1.19 acres)

This park is aptly named since it provides an excellent place to watch the sun go down over the bay. A footpath leads through a scenic wooded glade from the Fish Creek business section to this small park. You'll have a great view of Chambers Island from the park benches, but there is no parking available.

Clark Park (1.25 acres)

Since 1865 a dock has stood in the heart of Fish Creek welcoming vessels of all sizes and stature. In 1905 George M. Clark acquired the dock and refurbished the structure. The family later donated the dock and eventually the grounds which surround it to the town and it was named Clark Park. Today Clark Park and its adjacent dock are the center of activity during the various festivals that the village celebrates. A low stone wall along the bayshore surrounds the property, making swimming difficult. The adjacent dock accommodates about 30 boats. Fishermen are often found dangling bait or casting off the dock. Perch is the most popular target, but anglers also land an occasional trout, salmon or northern pike.

BOREAL FOREST
Boreas was the north wind god of the ancients. The boreal forest or taiga is the coniferous northern-most tree region around the world. The American boreal forest zone stretches from Maine across Canada to the Yukon and Alaska. Door County's boreal forest represents the southern-most extent of this zone.

Chambers Island Lighthouse Town Park (40 acres)

This Gibraltar town park offers visitors the only public access to Chambers Island and its wonderful beach. The dilapidated pier is no longer useful since it is not attached to shore. Boaters docking here will have to throw out an anchor and wade or take a dinghy to the beach. Surprisingly, there is a public access road running through the park, but vehicles are few on this isolated island. The lighthouse on the island is of historical significance.

Anderson Dock (25 acres)

Often the most luxurious yachts plying the peninsula are found docking at the twelve boat slips provided at Ephraim's Anderson Dock. The adjacent historic warehouse is now the site of the Hardy Memorial Art Gallery and the Anderson Store Museum.

Eagle Harbor offers an interesting insight into the seafaring past of this quaint village. It's also a convenient place to try fishing. Bass and perch are often caught right off the dock. A historic plaque placed by the Ephraim Foundation indicates the historical significance of this site. Parking is available.

Sister Bay Village Park (2 acres)

A guarded swimming beach and concrete pier complement the Sister Bay central business district at this village park. Located on Highway 42 (Bay Shore Drive), this public park and beach also offers a picnic shelter, swings and picnic tables. Parking is available for about 20 cars. It's best to arrive early in the day to avoid congestion.

Ellison Bluff County Park (88 acres)

Located off Highway 42 between the villages of Sister Bay and Ellison Bay, Ellison Bluff County Park sits upon wooded headlands. A stairway leads to a viewing site providing an awe-inspiring view of Green Bay waters. Access to Green Bay waters is all but impossible since a high limestone precipice separates the viewing site from the shore. There are picnic facilities and parking for about 15 cars.

Gateway Village Park (1.62 acres)

A tourist information cabin at the intersection of State Highways 42 and 57 stands as the gateway to Sister Bay. The cabin was constructed in 1866 and was restored in 1976 as a bicentennial restoration project. This is a convenient location to stretch your legs and plan your visit to Sister Bay.

Ephraim Village Playground (2.7 acres)

The Ephraim Village Playground is tucked away off County Q on a bluff above the downtown district. A basketball court, three tennis courts and playground equipment mark the location. This park is next to the grammar school and there is boat trailer parking available.

Sister Bay Athletic Field (6 acres)

Door County residents love watching their summer league baseball teams battle it out, and the Sister Bay Athletic Field is one of the locations where these matches take place. Located on North Highland Road, the field has bleacher stands to provide you with a place to sit while you enjoy a little summer baseball Door County-style.

Ellison Bay Women's Club Park (3 acres)

This park, also known as the Ellison Bay Community Center, has two swimming beaches separated by a dock. One of these two secluded beaches is sand and offers a great place to take a dip. The park also has two tennis courts, playground equipment, a meeting house and a pleasant lawn for relaxing. Parking is available on nearby streets.

Ellison Bay Men's Club Park (.6 acres)

This park is also known as Ellison Bay Town Park and offers two boat ramps, a 24-slip boat dock and considerable parking. It is centrally located off Highway 42.

(opposite page)
Lady slippers lay their claim to the forest floor at The Clearing, an adult "school of the soil" in Ellison Bay.

PRESERVES

Fuller Tract Natural Area

This preserve, also known as the Peninsula Center Sanctuary, is a 160-acre natural area located off County E, west of Egg Harbor. Two small stone monuments mark the eastern boundary of the property. Parking for one or two cars is available off the unmarked dirt road that parallels the northern border of the property.

FACILITIES:
A day-use area, this preserve is open year-round to explorers on foot or skis.

RECREATION:
Bird-watching, hiking, cross-country skiing.

An impressive stone fence reveals countless hours of laborious toil upon the abandoned farm fields of the Fuller Tract. Nature is reclaiming this land, just as Judson Fuller wished it would when he deeded the property to the University of Wisconsin in 1970. Fuller, a UW alumnus from River Forest, Illinois, put no restrictions on the property, but did request that it be left intact "as an outdoor nature laboratory for university students of botany, wildlife and ecology." To date, Fuller's wishes have been respected, and red pine, cedar, birch and maple trees are again gaining a hold in the rocky soil.

Also known as the Peninsula Center Sanctuary, naturalists from the nearby Ridges Sanctuary occasionally offer summer birding expeditions to this parcel, providing an excellent opportunity for further discovery. There is a sad footnote in the history of the Fuller Tract. A few days after the Fullers deeded the property to the University of Wisconsin Foundation, on December 18, 1970, they suffered a tragic auto accident. Judson Fuller's wife, Jessie, was killed and Mr. Fuller was critically injured. Today the Peninsula Center Sanctuary serves as a living memorial to Jessie Fuller and those who tilled the soil before her.

Crossroads at Big Creek
Historical and Environmental Preserve

Students enjoy the freedom of a classroom without walls at Crossroads at Big Creek Historical and Environmental Preserve in Sturgeon Bay. Located near Big Creek just over the Bayview Bridge on the east side of Sturgeon Bay, this 93-acre preserve was founded in 1991 as an environmental and historical education center. Hiking trails marked by bluebird boxes wind through the preserve past two wildlife ponds providing both bird-watching and cross-country skiing opportunities.

Uniquely, Crossroads is also home to the Leif Everson Astronomical Observatory and its 14-inch telescope. Open to both students and the public at large during "viewing nights," the computer controlled telescope is housed in a 10-foot dome offering a window to the universe.

History also plays a role in the preserve since it has become the home of the Vignes one-room schoolhouse. Built at the turn of the century, this schoolhouse was moved 11 miles to Crossroads from where it once stood in the Door County town of Clay Banks. Teachers plan to use the historic school as a learning tool. Students will be encouraged to take part in week-long sessions taught in the one-room schoolhouse where history will come to life.

FACILITIES:

A day-use area, this preserve is open year-round to foot traffic, skiing and snowshoeing. It is also home to the Leif Everson Astronomical Observatory.

RECREATION:

Star gazing, bird-watching, hiking, cross-country skiing.

BEACHES

Horseshoe Bay Beach
(Frank E. Murphy Beach)
This park is on Horseshoe Bay, 2.5 miles south of Egg Harbor. Take County G down the shoreline to County B. You'll find a great swimming beach, a concrete pier and an excellent view of Horseshoe Bay. There are picnic facilities and a boat ramp as well. The park is about 14 acres in size.

Egg Harbor Village Beach
A stone wall runs along the shore of this pebble beach. While the beach isn't sand, it does provide a nice view of the harbor and the village. Playground equipment can be found along the grass lawn, and an access road runs through the park grounds to private homes along the northern boundary. A resort forms the southern boundary. Across from the beach on County G a recently acquired 10-acre woodlot protects bedrock outcrops, glacial dune ridges and a small wetland.

Chambers Island Beach
You'll need a boat to reach the beach on Chambers Island but it's certainly worth the effort. Deep sand and lovely water will surround you at this 40-acre Town of Gibraltar preserve. Located on the northern shore of the island, this park is a popular spot for boaters to toss out an anchor. The lack of adequate docking facilities will require that you row, paddle or wade to shore. An airport runway is found behind the beach.

Ephraim Public Beach
The comfortable sand bottom of Eagle Harbor welcomes the tender feet of swimmers taking a dip at the Ephraim village beach. Several years ago, when Lake Michigan was undergoing a period of high water, this beach all but disappeared. Now that Lake Michigan has retreated the exposed beach is a great place to stretch out a blanket and enjoy the cliffs of Peninsula State Park, visible across Eagle Harbor.

LAKE LEVELS
Lake Michigan reached record high levels in 1986, causing severe erosion to the Peninsula State Park's seven miles of shoreline. During that year water levels were five feet above the water mark of 1969.

Fish Creek Village Beach

A marked swimming area, easy access and a commanding view of Peninsula State Park combine to draw hundreds of sun lovers to the Fish Creek Public Beach each summer. Drawn by swing sets and a shallow bay, this beach is a favorite destination of families vacationing on the peninsula. The shallow water here is often several degrees warmer than on the lakeshore, and brave youngsters can be found swimming here all summer long. The only way to beat the crowds is to arrive at dusk when the last traces of daylight flee across the moored sailboats and even the hardiest beachgoers retire.

Nicolet Bay Beach

Nicolet Bay Beach is often crowded, but that's because it's one of the best beaches on the peninsula. The beach commands a stunning view of Nicolet Bay and Horseshoe Island. The water here is often warmer than elsewhere on the bay side because the shallow water absorbs the sun's heat and holds it. This is also a central meeting spot for boaters on the peninsula, and the grounds behind the beach have been the site of many frisbee, football and volleyball games. Parents will find play equipment for their children, and sailboats, canoes, kayaks, sailboards and bicycles may be rented during the summer. The swimming area is well marked. Once at Peninsula State Park, follow Shore Road from the park's Fish Creek entrance—you can't miss it.

Sister Bay Village Beach

Sister Bay offers one of the few guarded beaches on the Door Peninsula. The nearby dock and pleasant surroundings bring a bustle of activity to this beach during summer.

Ellison Bay Women's Park Beach

This small beach is rarely crowded and the surrounding grounds provide excellent picnicking opportunities. A dock separates the pebble beach from the sand beach. Tennis courts are found nearby.

BICYCLE TOURS

Egg Harbor—Heartland Tour

This tour begins along a cliff before winding through the Door County heartland to Kangaroo Lake, where swimming is available, before the return to Egg Harbor.

Begin this trek at the village dock in Egg Harbor and follow the bayshore up White Cliff Road. Parts of this ride traverse terrain that is moderate to steep, but the views from the bluffs are worth the effort. So, climb the cliff and cross Highway 42. You're now on Juddville Road. Take Juddville Road to County A. Turn right on A. This takes you past the farms and fields of northern Door County. Continue on A as it crosses County EE and County E until you reach Wooded Lane. Cross Wooded Lane and take the next left on Beach Road. Beach Road dead ends at a public access to Kangaroo Lake. To continue, with the lake at your back, turn

EGG HARBOR–
HEARTLAND
BICYCLE TOUR

Egg Harbor–Heartland Tour

- - - - BICYCLE ROUTE (19 MILES)

right on the first road from the water. This is Kangaroo Lake Road. Take this road to the stop sign and turn left. Heading up the hill you'll bear right at the sign for Logerquist Road. This road becomes County E. Heading down E you'll find a stone marker commemorating the Fuller Tract Peninsula Sanctuary. Remain on E and you'll intersect with Highway 42 just north of the village limits.

Bicyclists travel the Sunset Bike Trail on a ribbon of limestone scree which winds through Peninsula State Park.

Sunset Tour (9 miles)

The tour winds through Peninsula State Park on the Sunset Bike Trail, providing five miles of traffic-free travel over limestone screenings before connecting with paved park roads. The ride begins just south of the park's visitor contact station. You'll encounter two-way traffic (bicycles) as you begin this loop so be on the lookout. Soon you'll be crossing a causeway over a beautiful marsh, then hug the bossier for an outstanding view of Green Bay.

Just south of the Tennison Bay Campground you'll reach the new Hidden Bluff spur trail which leads to the White Cedar Nature Center. This short (.75 mile) trail is credited with doubling the number of visitors to the park's nature center.

The trail takes you near the Nicolet Bay Beach. After arriving at the beach follow the bike trail markers along Shore Road where you'll pass the overflow parking lot and the Vita Course en route to paved Hemlock Road. Follow Hemlock Road to Middle Road and bear right to return to the Sunset Trail. Turn left on the Sunset Trail at the top of the hill after you pass Blossomburg Cemetery, and you'll be heading back to the trailhead. The terrain is moderate, but please note that you'll be sharing the Sunset Trail with other cyclists, wheelchair users and white-tailed deer. The tour uses about four miles of roads where you might encounter cars.

Peninsula Mountain Bike Jaunt

If you're 16 or older you'll need a trail pass (available at the park office). These trails serve cross-country skiers in winter forming several loops that can be combined with paved roads for a full-day outing without leaving the park. Helmets are, of course, mandatory since some of the hills are steep and the terrain rugged. The intersections are well marked with "you are here" signs so bikers will not have trouble navigating this exciting new addition to the Peninsula Park outdoor scene.

MOUNTAIN
BIKING
PENINSULA
STATE PARK
Since the early 1900s Peninsula State Park has added eight miles of off-road trail for mountain bikers. Riders using these trails must first purchase a state park trail pass.

Peninsula Park Backroads (9.5 miles)

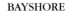

Peninsula State Park's backroads wind through a forested preserve tailor-made for bike riding. To reduce congestion on the park's popular Sunset Trail, park officials have expanded Shore Road along a one-mile stretch from the park office. This widened route begins at the Visitor Center and winds over Weborg Marsh before connecting to Mengleberg Lane. A right turn on Mengleberg Lane avoids congested Shore Road and brings bicyclists into the heart of the park. Another right turn on Middle Road will link bikers to the park's marked Sunset Bicycle Trail, but keep in mind sections of this trail are not paved. To remain on paved roads and follow the Peninsula Backroads tour, ignore the green bicycle signs and turn left on Middle Road. At intersection of Skyline Road turn right for a long, gradual climb up to Sven's Bluff. Remain on Skyline through the intersection with Hemlock and proceed up another smaller hill before winding down with a view of Nicolet Bay below you. At Highland Road turn right to Middle Road. Stay on Middle Road through its intersection with Hemlock and you'll return to Mengleberg Lane and the Blossomburg Cemetery for your trip back back to the Visitor Center.

CANOE AND KAYAK ROUTES

Eagle Harbor Excursion

To get to Eagle Harbor, take Highway 42 to Ephraim and put in at the Ephraim public boat landing. Beginners should hug the shoreline where the village provides a picturesque background as you paddle along admiring the beautiful summer homes lining this natural harbor. Directly across the harbor are the limestone cliffs of Peninsula State Park. Experts may wish to paddle across the bay to explore the cliffs and caves. This is a good place to cool off at the public swimming beach south of the boat landing.

Horseshoe Island

To get to the put-in at Peninsula State Park, follow Shore Road to Nicolet Bay Beach. This trip offers wooded undeveloped shoreline, towering cliffs and Lake Michigan islands.

From Nicolet Bay Beach, it's a two-mile paddle to Horseshoe Island. This 38-acre sanctuary was once called Eagle Island, but its natural harbor and unique shape led to the name change. Administered as part of Peninsula State Park, the island serves as a picnic area for paddlers and a protected harbor for sailors. This trip merits an expert rating in an open canoe because once you hit open water beyond Nicolet Bay, swells can develop that aren't recognizable from shore. The crossing is somewhat less of a challenge for kayakers, and those wishing to continue island hopping can round the point on the western shore of the mainland to the Strawberry Islands. These islands are privately held. Navigation chart: NOAA #14909.

Chambers Island

The put-in for this open water crossing is the Tennison Bay Boat Landing at Peninsula State Park. Follow Shore Road from the Peninsula State Park entrance to Tennison Bay Campground.

The Strawberry Islands, which include Pirate, Jack, Little Strawberry and Adventure islands, provide the only protection between Peninsula State Park and Chambers Island for kayakers planning this ambitious day trip. Chambers Island lies six miles from shore. A former Coast Guard lighthouse station on the northwest corner of the island is now a 40-acre day-use park that includes a small beach with picnic facilities for day paddlers. Sea kayakers en route to Michigan will find this park a convenient resting place.

The historic Island Lighthouse retired along with the last lighthouse keeper in 1950. The rest of the island is privately owned.

This trip is for expert sea kayakers. Navigation chart: NOAA #14909.

CITIES, TOWNS AND VILLAGES

The Village of Egg Harbor (pop. 230)

Limestone bluffs rise to protect the natural bay at Egg Harbor from the fierce and often unpredictable storms that occasionally blow over the waters of Green Bay. Perhaps it was this protection that tempted Levi and Jacob Thorp in 1855 to purchase 1,600 acres where the village now stands. After constructing a dock, the pair took up the cordwood business, following in the footsteps of a third brother, Asa Thorp. Asa was already supplying cordwood to ships docking at his pier in Fish Creek. Business boomed, but Levi caught a touch of gold fever and headed for California to stake his claim in the gold fields. When he returned, his pockets bulged with some $5,000 in gold dust, making him one of the wealthiest businessmen north of Sturgeon Bay. To celebrate his good fortune he constructed the historic "Cupola House" in 1871. To this day it remains one of the most impressive buildings in the village.

Tales vary as to how Egg Harbor was christened. One story, related by Elizabeth Fisher Baird, wife of a famous Green Bay attorney, claims the harbor received its name following a playful bout in 1825 during which eggs were used as ammunition in a mock naval battle. Says Baird, "We began to see eggs flying in the air . . . I crawled under the tarpaulin, where I was comparatively safe, although an occasional egg would strike me on the head." A less colorful version holds that peninsula pioneer Increase Claflin named the harbor after finding a nest of duck eggs on the shore of the bay. Claflin is also credited with naming Fish Creek, Horseshoe Bay, Hat Island, the Strawberry Islands and Eagle (Horseshoe) Island, lending further credence to the origin of the village name.

After reaching a peak population of over 1,000 residents in 1910, Egg Harbor is home to only about 230 year-round residents today. Once considered a stepping stone to Fish Creek, Egg Harbor has bolstered its tourist trade by revamping the village with quaint storefronts and tasteful development. Today the village has firmly established itself as a resort destination with

THE CUPOLA HOUSE

The Cupola House was built in 1871 by Levi Thorp. Today it remains an Egg Harbor landmark and the most striking example of Gothic Revival-style architecture in Door County.

BLOSSOMBERG,
"THE WINDY
MOUNTAIN"
Ole Klunseland, an early settler to Door County, called the area near Fish Creek where he made his home Blossomberg, meaning "the windy mountain." The name was apparently derived from the peculiar winds caused by the meeting of water, bluff and forests. Today most traces of this early settlement have vanished but a town cemetary within Peninsula State Park retains the Blossomberg name.

a sprinkling of orchards and dairy farms in the surrounding countryside.

Unfortunately, condominiums have begun to claw into the irreplaceable escarpment forest south of the village where one of the geologic wonders of the peninsula can be found in a fissure of rock known as Tecumseh Cave. The cave is over 1,750 feet long, the longest cave known in Wisconsin. It was discovered by local hunters in 1879. Located on private property, the cave is open only to qualified individuals with a legitimate scientific interest. The owners and a few members of the Wisconsin Speleologic Society have explored the cave, but to date no one has reached its conclusion. The cave takes its name from the legend surrounding an Indian chief named Tecumseh. It is said that soldiers were pursuing the sly chief when he ducked into the cave. A guard was stationed at the entrance, but Tecumseh never emerged. He was reportedly seen alive and well later on, having eluded his would-be captors. A second entrance to the cave has never been discovered.

Egg Harbor Village Beach: The beach is located at the south end of the village. Exit Highway 42 at County G. The small pebble beach has a great view of Egg Harbor.

Village Dock and Park: This launch site is off Dock Road, in the center of Egg Harbor. Take Highway 42 to Dock Road. In addition to a boat ramp, the 2-acre park offers a pier and picnic facilities.

Frank E. Murphy County Park: This 14-acre park is on Horseshoe Bay, 2.5 miles south of Egg Harbor. Take County G down the shoreline to County B. You'll find a great swimming beach, a concrete pier, and an excellent view of Horseshoe Bay. There are picnic facilities and a boat ramp as well.

Library: The library at Egg Harbor is off Highway 42 in the village. The phone: 920-868-3334.

Birch Creek Music Center: In addition to gorgeous

scenery, this is one of the extras Door County offers to enhance its claim as a vacation paradise. During the summer, students from the Birch Creek Music Center perform free concerts in the gazebo of the Cupola House in Egg Harbor. If one of these concerts whets your appetite for more, Birch Creek students perform nearby in a rustic but comfortable barn from late June to mid-August. For reservations write: P.O. Box 230, Egg Harbor, WI 54209, or call: 920-868-3763.

Fourth of July: Another event worth attending is the Fourth of July parade, which finds tourists and locals alike lining the highway as floats pass, marking another summer in Door County.

The Village of Fish Creek (pop. 250)

The gentle descent down Highway 42 into the village of Fish Creek brings visitors to the heart of the northern Door Peninsula. Plans by the Wisconsin Department of Transportation in 1987 to dynamite this spectacular bluff in the interest of highway safety were met with such vehement opposition by local residents that modifications were made to preserve the road's scenic integrity.

Increase Claflin was the first white settler to stake a claim in Fish Creek arriving in 1842, although Asa Thorp is credited with founding the village. He constructed a dock here and initiated a commercial cordwood enterprise in 1853. What remains of Thorp's cabin still stands near Founder's Square among the shops and galleries that today provide the center of commerce in the village.

In the early 1850s, Peter Weborg and Even Nelson led several families to settle land near here in the area now called Weborg Point within Peninsula State Park. Life for these settlers was a challenge. Since the rock soil was too thin to farm, many soon turned to the bounty of the lake where abundant whitefish and herring provided a livelihood. Others planted vineyards on the Strawberry Islands off Tennison Bay and still others established apple and cherry orchards.

FOUNDER'S SQUARE
In the heart of Fish Creek, the complex of shops, restaurants and galleries is known collectively as "Founder's Square." The buildings were originally part of a summer hotel and cottage resort operated by Edgar Thorp.

A squall rolls into Fish Creek.

By the late 1860s Fish Creek was a bustling fishing and lumbering village. Asa Thorp was one of the first to recognize the tourist potential of the area and in the 1860s he built a small hotel which grew to accommodate 125 summer guests in 1896.

About this time Dr. Herman Welcker purchased one mile of shoreline from Thorp and began developing a health resort. To accommodate guests, Welcker moved several intact buildings across the winter ice of Green Bay from economically depressed Marinette, Wisconsin and Menominee, Michigan to Fish Creek.

Today, the memory of these entrepreneurs are invoked by campers making their way to the campgrounds which bear the names Welckers and Weborg within Peninsula State Park.

Fish Creek itself was once a rich spawning area for fish. But when timber was stripped from its banks, erosion took its toll and the once-navigable stream today is barely deep enough for a canoe. Strides are being made to protect the stream, however. Recently, the state of Wisconsin purchased a portion of the stream bank, adding the acreage to Peninsula State Park.

Visitors should not miss the scenic drive down Cottage Row. Here are some of the most exclusive summer "cottages" on the peninsula. It's fun to imagine owning one of these regal retreats, but the view from your tent on Nicolet Bay is even better than theirs.

Fish Creek, with a permanent population of about 250, offers a library and a civic association. The library, off Highway 42, offers tourist information as well as library services. The phone: 920-868-3471. The address of the civic association: Box 1974, Fish Creek, WI 54212.

A number of "must see" cultural events await summer visitors to this village. Of particular note are performances by the Peninsula Players at the "Theatre in a Garden," classical music performances during the Peninsula Music Festival, and the American Folklore Theatre performances held in the amphitheater of Peninsula State Park.

The Peninsula Players: Touted as the world's oldest professional resident summer theater, the players perform in a peaceful open-air bayshore setting with a relaxed rural atmosphere. In 1995 it celebrated its 60th anniversary. For information or reservations phone: 920-868-3287

The Peninsula Music Festival: The Peninsula Music Festival has brought top-caliber classical musicians to Fish Creek for several weeks each August since 1953. Sponsored by the Peninsula Arts Association, the festival is the highlight of the summer for those combining a love of classical music with their love of the Door Peninsula. For information phone: 920-854-4060.

American Folklore Theatre: This delightful entourage of musicians both educate and entertain during July and August at Peninsula State Park's amphitheater. These family-oriented folk productions mix music with history in an outdoor setting, creating a combination that's hard to beat. Times are posted on the park bulletin boards, or call the park's visitor center for information.

The Peninsula Dance Program: Those wishing to hone their dancing skills will enjoy the Peninsula Dance Program offered by the University of Wisconsin Division of Continuing Studies, Liberal Studies and the Arts. Summer dance classes and performances are offered. For information and fees phone: 608-263-8927

The Peninsula Art School: Watercolor and oil painting has always been the main focus of the Peninsula Art School but classes run the gamut from paper making to pioneer pottery. All ages and skill levels are welcome to take part in the classes which run from June through October. For more information phone: 920-868-3455.

Sunset Town Park: This small park is three blocks west of the Highway 42 stop sign where Main Street meets Green Bay. It offers a sunset view of Chambers Island.

Clark Memorial Town Park: Another small park on the bay, this is a nice place to pretend you own one of the yachts visible from here.

Chambers Island Town Park: This island is about four miles offshore and is accessible by boat only. There's a pier on the east side where you can tie up, or you can drag your kayak up the sand beach. It's a day-use park only, but this 40-acre site makes a nice isolated spot for a picnic.

The Village of Ephraim (pop. 309)

If Fish Creek represents the heart of the northern Door Peninsula, Ephraim marks its soul. It is amid the white buildings and bluff-side churches on the sparkling bay that visitors develop a passion for this area and a longing to preserve it.

An unwritten law requiring that buildings in Ephraim be painted white or carry no paint at all has survived since the early Moravians settled on this harbor in the 1850s. You won't find a pub in this village either. As if not to tarnish the lily-white appearance of Ephraim, the village remains dry.

Across the harbor, one can see 180-foot-high Eagle Bluff. For years a pair of eagles nested near this site and may have been responsible for the name given to this bay, Eagle Harbor. Eagles have made a recent return to Door County and once again they can be seen soaring above the bay and bluffs. Horseshoe Island (formerly called Eagle Island) lies in the harbor. The natural U-shaped harbor on Horseshoe Island is said to have provided refuge to French explorer Jean Nicolet in 1630. Today it serves the same function for modern-day adventurers who drop anchor to admire the view or spend the night.

Scandinavian immigrants were also drawn to this village due to its resemblance to their homeland. Ephraim's Fyr (pronounced "fear") Ball Festival pays tribute to this heritage during a celebration marking the summer solstice. Bonfires are lit along the shore at dusk during a ceremony commemorating the arrival of summer with the burning of the winter witch. A local dignitary is crowned Fyr Ball Chieftan and a traditional fish boil rounds out the evening's entertainment.

Just south of the village lies the north entrance to Peninsula State Park and one of the most beautiful golf courses in the Midwest. Teeing off from limestone bluffs, golfers will enjoy both the challenge and the beauty surrounding them on this 18-hole course. An errant five iron may well land near the fairway totem pole that marks the 1931 burial site of Potawatomi Chief Khaquados. Chief Khaquados was a direct descendant of Chief Onanquisse, a Potawatomi credited with saving the lives of starving French explorers as they wintered on the peninsula in 1680. Chief Khaquados was said to have been so pleased with the totem pole, erected before his death, that he remarked, "This is the first time the white man not only

EPHRAIM ANCESTRY

Ephraim's history can be traced to the fjords of Norway. Early Moravians of Norwegian descent settled in Ephraim in 1853 and later built summer hotels to attract visitors.

kept his word, but has done more than he promised."

Ephraim shares an airport with the town of Gibraltar. It's located on Maple Grove Road south of Ephraim.

EPHRAIM SWAMP
The Ephraim Swamp originally began at the Green Bay shore in Ephraim and extended to the floor of the bluff in Gibraltar Township. As development encroached on the area, the bayshore section was drained, filled and developed.

Library/Village Hall: Located on Highway 42 where it curves in downtown Ephraim. Phone: 920-854-2014.

Ephraim Information Center: For information write the center at Ephraim, WI 54211. Phone: 920-854-2014.

Anderson Museum: This is located on the north end of the village on Highway 42.

Anderson Dock Park: Located off Highway 42 at the north end of the village. There are boat slips here and a place for fishing, all with a great view of the Peninsula State Park bluffs.

Ephraim Playground: At the corner of Norway and Church streets you'll find tennis courts, a basketball court, playground equipment and picnic tables.

Ephraim Village Beach: The beach is off Highway 42 at the south end of the village. It's a sand beach with parking and has a nice view of the harbor.

A Walking Tour of Ephraim

Ephraim's rich history comes to life as you take a walking tour through the village. Beginning at the village hall in the center of town, a brief hike north along the bayshore will bring you to Anderson's Dock. Here, in 1859, Aaslag Anderson and a Mr. Peter Peterson purchased 150 acres from the Moravian church for $200. These two men built the dock and later the general store that served as the center of activity in this village. Today, the rustic building adjacent to the dock is painted with the various ship names that have docked here over the years, providing an interesting spectacle. The building houses the Francis Hardy Art Gallery, which is operated by a group of Ephraim residents as an art center. The Hardy Gallery is open to the public at designated hours.

Across from the dock you'll find the old Anderson Homestead, which has recently been restored.

To continue your tour, walk up the hill to the east to Moravia Street. Turning right you'll be taking a picturesque walk through an arch of cedar and white birch leading to the Pioneer Schoolhouse. This village schoolhouse was built in 1869 and operated by the Ephraim Foundation as a museum open to the public. During summer this building houses the office of the Peninsula Music Festival. Nearby you'll find the Goodletson family homestead, dating back to the 1860s. Next to the Pioneer Schoolhouse is the Lutheran Church.

A winding walk north up County Q will bring you to Ephraim's present-day kindergarten and the village tennis and basketball courts. Continue south down Norway Street to Valentine Lane and you'll find the Moravian cemetery. A glimpse at the old monuments will open a chapter in Ephraim's past.

Heading down the hill again towards the bay will take you to the Ephraim Moravian Church, noted for its white steeple. The church, originally 40 feet by 24 feet by 16 feet in height, was moved from the shore to its present site. South of the Moravian parsonage is the site of Pastor Iverson's original home. Now in private ownership, the original limestone drywall in front of the home was built by Iverson himself.

A walk south along the shore takes you to the Ephraim public beach. You'll have a great view of the village and limestone cliffs of Peninsula State Park across the bay. Returning to the center of the village you'll pass a stone monument marking the first landing of Iverson and his Moravian followers. From here it's a short trip back to the village hall, which houses the public library. This impressive building reflects the Scandinavian heritage of Ephraim and provides an excellent vantage point to watch the sunset over Eagle Harbor.

Village of Sister Bay (pop. 696)

The village of Sister Bay lies in the shelter of the Sister Bluffs. These twin cliffs rise 130 and 190 feet above the bayshore, towering over a second pair of siblings in the bay called the Sister Islands.

This is the largest and busiest village north of Sturgeon Bay, and many of its current residents trace their roots to Scandinavians who settled this region in the 1860s. Among the Swedes who came was a massive woodcutter by the name of John A. "Long John" Johnson. Known for his insatiable appetite, legend has it that a local storekeeper bet the giant five dollars he couldn't eat five dozen eggs in one sitting. Long John took the bet on the condition the prize included a pint of whiskey. Long John is said to have eaten all the eggs, drunk the whiskey and gone home to top it off with a loaf of bread and a pail of milk.

As ax gave way to plow, woodcutters who chose to stay in Sister Bay took up either fishing or farming. On the Door Peninsula fishing was a year-round affair with fishermen making their way across the ice to cast their nets. The danger of this practice was illustrated in 1893, when nine men sailed their ice sleds about five miles across the unpredictable frozen bay. Wind sent the fishing party adrift on the bay when an ice floe broke from the mainland. Rescue by boat was hampered by high winds, and the nine were given up for dead. But three days later the wind shifted, and the ice floe was spotted on the horizon making its way toward shore. Near enough to jump for land, the fishermen were saved by the same cursed wind that had sent them sailing.

Today, Sister Bay is the center of population and commerce on the northern Door Peninsula. During summer its streets are filled with tourists shopping and gawking at the goats atop a local sod-roofed restaurant. Autumn finds people converging on Sister Bay during Fall Fest, held annually during the third weekend in October. This is one of the busiest festivals on the Door Peninsula and reservations are highly recommended.

Despite the bustling streets and throngs of tourists, wildlife still manages to carve a niche just beyond the village limits. The 1988 harvest of a black bear by a Sister Bay bow hunter in northern Door County confirms this. Even though the bruin was taken legally, its death still ruffled the feathers of residents opposed to sanctioned hunting of the very few bears still roaming wild in Door County.

Gateway Park: At the intersection of Highways 42 and 57, look for the log cabin housing the tourist information center. There is also a picnic area.

Sister Bay Advancement Association: For information write: P.O. Box 201, Sister Bay, WI 54234, or phone: 920-854-2812.

Sister Bay Village Park: Off Highway 42 in the center of town, this park offers a guarded sand and pebble beach and a dock.

Sand Bay Town Park: This 5-acre park is located four miles northeast of Sister Bay. Take Highway 42 to Waters End Road, turn right (east) to North Sand Bay Lane. There's a beach on Lake Michigan that's perfect for launching a sea kayak.

Pebble Beach: Take Pebble Beach Road off Highway 42 at the southwestern edge of the village. As the name implies, this is a pebble, not sand, beach.

Village of Ellison Bay

Ellison Bay unfolds like a beautiful painting as visitors arriving from the south crest 190-foot-high Ellison Bluff overlooking this quaint village. En route from Sister Bay, orchards fill the landscape with blossoms in late May, making this a perfect time to visit the tip of the peninsula.

Founded by John Ellison, a Dane who moved up the bayshore from Ephraim to make his fortune in 1863, the village has a long and rich history of catering to tourists. The annual Olde Ellison Bay Days celebration in late June continues this tradition with a rope pull, parade and fish boil. The simple recipe of fresh whitefish, potatoes and onions has been a Door Peninsula tradition since fishermen began casting their nets in these waters over a century ago.

Hiking either the Mink River Nature Conservancy or nearby Newport State Park is a great way to burn off the calories gained enjoying the whitefish feast.

Open to passive recreation, including hiking and cross-country skiing, both of these preserves demand delicate exploration.

The Clearing: A drive through Ellison Bay is not complete until motorists wind down scenic Garrett Bay Road, and if it's a Saturday or Sunday afternoon, a visit to The Clearing should be high on your agenda. Long one of the best-kept secrets in Door County, The Clearing is the legacy of Chicago-based landscape architect Jens Jenson. This native Dane, at age 75, envisioned a "school of the soil" where aspiring landscape architects could gain hands-on experience at this 125-acre bluffs-edge site located on the northern end of Ellison Bay. The Clearing celebrated its 60th anniversary in 1995 and offers classes in music, writing, nature studies, dance and literature. Far removed from the neighboring beaches, gift shops and campgrounds, students spend their evenings in limestone and wood dormitories free of television but filled with contemplation. The Clearing is open to visitors on Saturday and Sunday afternoons, mid-May through October. Phone: 920-854-4088 or write: Box 65, Ellison Bay, WI 545210.

Ellison Bluff County Park: Three miles southwest of Ellison Bay on Highway 42, exit west on Porcupine Bay Road. Turn right on Ellison Bluff Road to the park. There's a spectacular view of Green Bay from the crest of Ellison Bluff. The 88-acre park also offers short hiking trails and picnic facilities.

Ellison Bay Municipal Dock and Ramp: This launch facility is off Highway 42 at the center of the village.

Ellison Bay Women's Club Park: Off Highway 42 at the south end of the village, this park offers a small beach, tennis courts and picnic facilities.

PIONEER STORE
The Pioneer Store is an Ellison Bay landmark. It was built in 1900 by Charles Ruckert and served as the village post office when Mr. Ruckert was postmaster from 1903 to 1915. Its current owners have maintained its rustic atmosphere and timeless appeal.

Europe Bay Town Park: Exit Highway 42 northeast of the village at Europe Bay Road and continue to the road's gravel conclusion. There's an excellent sand beach and picnic facilities, although parking is limited.

Newport State Park: Exit Highway 42 northeast of the village and follow the signs. There's a great beach here amid a wilderness setting.

LAKESHORE

EUROPE LAKE BEACH
EUROPE BAY TOWN PARK
NEWPORT STATE PARK
MINK RIVER ESTUARY
SAND BAY TOWN PARK & BEACH
TOWN OF LIBERTY GROVE SCHOOL FOREST
MARSHALL'S POINT NATURAL AREA
MUD LAKE WILDLIFE AREA
RIDGES SANCTUARY
TOFT POINT NATURE CONSERVANCY
BOES TOWN PARK
BAILEYS HARBOR RIDGES
COUNTY PARK & BEACH
BAILEYS HARBOR FIRE STATION FIELD
ANCLAM TOWN PARK & BEACH
BAILEYS HARBOR RECREATION FIELD
LYLE-HARTER-MATTER SANCTUARY
COUNTY PARK
MERIDIAN COUNTY PARK
LAKESIDE TOWN PARK & BEACH
JACKSONPORT COMMUNITY TOWN PARK
SCHAUER TOWN PARK & BEACH
CAVE POINT COUNTY PARK
WHITEFISH DUNES STATE PARK
WHITEFISH DUNES BEACH

STATE PARKS
TOWN, VILLAGE & COUNTY PARKS
PRESERVES
BEACHES

Through the Windshield

AN OVERVIEW OF THE LAKESHORE

Sand dunes, wetlands, rocky ledges and isolated bays characterize Door County's untamed lakeshore. State parks, private preserves, islands and lighthouses provide the variety of scenery that keeps visitors returning year after year. Lacking the commercial development of the bayshore, lakeshore visitors tend to appreciate the cooler temperatures and wild shores that harbor rare orchids, waterfowl and coyote.

From Sturgeon Bay, lakeshore travelers will be following Highway 57 along Lake Michigan. You'll wish to bring a sweater along on this trek since the lakeshore is frequently as much as ten degrees cooler than the bay side of the peninsula. If you're wishing to depart the well-traveled path, exit Highway 57 at County T, which leads to Glidden Drive. This is one of the most scenic drives in Door County and borders one of the last remaining privately held roadless areas on the peninsula. A number of dead-end roads with names like Deerpath and Arrowhead lanes provide public access to the lakeshore beach. In many cases, however, only the width of the road is public domain, so if you wish to take a walk down the beach, plan to get your feet wet to avoid trespassing on private property. Glidden Drive passes over Shivering Sands Creek, so named because the sand is said to quiver or "shiver" in the wind. This creek, fed by Maple Creek, drains Dunes Lake, one of the richest privately owned wetlands on the peninsula. Dunes Lake is a shallow drainage occupying an area submerged by ancient glacial Lake Nippissing. Nearly 400 acres of wooded swampland border this lake, extending to the Lake Michigan shore.

The Nature Conservancy has taken an interest in this important natural area and acquisition of property from willing sellers has begun. This private land conservation group is best known in Door County for its efforts in protecting Mink River Estuary located north of here near Rowley's Bay.

LAKE MICHIGAN

Lake Michigan is a freshwater lake with a maximum depth of 840 feet. Bottom types along Door County are predominantly bedrock, on exposed shores, and sand within the bayheads and shallow areas.

(overleaf)

The Upper Range Light, erected in 1869, is one of a pair of beacons which provided a line of sight to guide ships past the treacherous sand bars of Baileys Harbor. This one served as home to the resident light keeper.

Continuing north on Glidden Drive you'll pass over Whitefish Bay Creek. This picturesque creek drains Clark Lake. Bass, walleye, northern and perch constitute the fishery here and, if you're anxious to get your canoe wet, this 864-acre lake beckons. Just past Whitefish Bay Creek you'll reach the entrance to Whitefish Dunes State Park. If it's July or August, plan on taking a swim. You'll find the best beach on the peninsula awaiting you. Be advised, however, that Lake Michigan water levels have reached record heights in recent years forcing the closure of this beach to protect the fragile sand dunes from erosion by summer beach-goers. Don't worry, there's more to this park than a beautiful beach. Travelers will also discover out-standing hiking trails complete with planked walkways to assist in climbing the 90-foot-high sand dunes. These sand dunes separate Lake Michigan from Clark Lake. Clark Lake was once a bay of Lake Michigan but over time sand bars became sand dunes. As the wind swept these tiny building blocks inland an isthmus of sand was created. This isthmus separated the bay from Lake Michigan, creating Clark Lake. Grasses stabilized these sand dunes allowing other plants to take root and today the western side of the dunes are largely covered with trees and shrubs. The park protects a substantial portion of the southern shoreline on Clark Lake as well as the Lake Michigan frontage. Winter visitors will find scenic, mellow, cross-county ski trails and often the best snow conditions on the peninsula at Whitefish Dunes, thanks to the influence of Lake Michigan on winter storm patterns.

Travelers without the time or energy to follow Glidden Drive will find a clearly marked access road off Highway 57 leading to Whitefish Dunes State Park. Less than one mile from the Whitefish Dunes entrance, sandwiched between state park land, is Cave Point County Park. The thunderous waves of Lake Michigan have worn sea caves in the 30-foot-high cliff, and the landscape is inspiring regardless of the season. Since this is a county park, you won't need a state park sticker to park your car here to enjoy a picnic or begin a cross-country ski outing.

WHITEFISH DUNES TROLLING
The near-shore areas of Lake Michigan adjacent to Whitefish Dunes State Park provide excellent fishing. Trolling and surf casting in April and May are popular methods of fishing for brown, brook and rainbow trout.

BJORKLUNDEN VID SJON

The Boynton estate, the complete name of which is "Bjorklunden Vid Sjon," or "Brich Forest by the Water," includes the Boyntons' residence, the family chapel, a workshop, a studio and a caretaker's home. The buildings are situated on 325 acres of wooded land fronting Lake Michigan.

From the entrance of Whitefish Dunes State Park, scenic Cave Point Drive leads to Highway 57 just south of Jacksonport. Jacksonport is located on the 45th Meridian, halfway between the North Pole and the Equator. Some 300 years ago, this area was a large Potawatomi Indian village known as Mechingan. When settlers arrived here in the mid-1800s, the great cedar forests that sheltered the Potawatomi fell to the ax and saw of logger Andrew Jackson, for whom the village is named.

Today, Jacksonport is a pleasant lakeshore farming community with a fine sand beach that has attracted many vacation home owners. Most of the families who settled this region are of German ancestry, and they celebrate this heritage with the annual "Maifest." Lakeside Park is the center of Maifest activities, offering an excellent sand beach and plenty of room to polka.

Driving through the dense evergreen stand between Jacksonport and Baileys Harbor you'll pass over Hibbards Creek. Fishermen are attracted to its steel-head trout runs. Having driven 21 miles from Sturgeon Bay, you'll now be entering Baileys Harbor. Once a logging camp, shipping point and original Door County seat, Baileys Harbor is today a popular resort community. The village is named after Captain Justice Bailey, who took refuge in its natural harbor in 1844. Today, fishing captains frequently launch their own excursions from this village, hoping to battle a chinook salmon, coho or trout.

Just south of the village, off Highway 57 you'll find the entrance to Lawrence University's extensive lakeshore holdings and the famed Bjorklunden Chapel. This "sanctuary of peace" was hand-crafted in Norwegian-style architecture from 1939–47 by Winifred and Donald Boynton. Today the chapel and grounds are maintained by Lawrence University and open Monday and Wednesday afternoons from 1–4 from mid-June through August. Bjorklunden is also home to week-long educational seminars sponsored by the Appleton, Wisconsin, based liberal arts college. The spectrum of subjects ranges from history to nature study. Phone 920-839-2216.

At the north end of Baileys Habor off Ridges Drive, a lovely sand beach invites a swim. This county park is adjacent to the world-renowned Ridges Sanctuary. The entrance to this private wildflower preserve can be found just north of Ridges Drive off Highway 57. The 900-acre natural garden is open to the public and protects some 17 wooded sand "ridges" and the wet swales that lie between them. These ancient ridges harbor over 25 species of orchids and rare flowers such as the dwarf iris, arctic primrose and fringed gentian. Located on the Ridges Sanctuary is a pair of famous old rangelights providing a line of sight to guide ships into the harbor. These two synchronized beacons were built in 1870, replacing the original Baileys Harbor lighthouse that had served the port since 1852. The old rangelight residence once served as home to Ridges' naturalist Roy Lukes. In 1975 the old wooden light tower was completely restored by the Sanctuary, but today modern navigational aids have rendered the historic beacons obsolete.

Adjacent to Ridges Sanctuary, off Ridges Road, is Toft Point Nature Conservancy. This magnificent 633-acre preserve encompasses virgin forest and untamed shoreline. In 1976, the University of Wisconsin, which administrates the property, attempted to have the gravel road winding through this site abandoned by the town to prevent motorized intrusion. To date this hasn't occurred and while a drive is still possible, hiking or skiing remains the best means of exploration.

Rolling out of Baileys Harbor you'll have the option of cruising down County Q through a remote and intriguing portion of the peninsula. This pleasant road snakes through the Ridges Sanctuary, following Moonlight Bay before crossing Riebolts Creek. Before spilling into Lake Michigan, this stream drains Mud Lake, a 155-acre shallow pool surrounded by wetlands, cedar and aspen groves. Combined with adjacent Ridges Sanctuary and Toft Point, this ecosystem has been designated a national landmark. Mud Lake is also a state wildlife area. Penetrating this rugged land can be difficult, adding to its unique appeal. Continuing down Q you'll encounter the side road leading to Cana

Island. A stone causeway, accessible by foot, makes Cana the most accessible of all Door County islands. A historic lighthouse awaits you. Built in 1869, this working lighthouse still warns ships of treacherous offshore reefs. The grounds and keeper's house are leased from the Coast Guard by the Door County Maritime Museum which offers tours mid-May through October from 10–5.

Near Cana Island, east of Highway Q, lies the Baileys Harbor Boreal Forest and the Moonlight Bay Bedrock State Natural Areas. These two areas are among the largest remaining tracts of undeveloped Lake Michigan shoreline in Wisconsin.

The boundaries to the 1,180-acre Boreal Forest State Natural Area were approved in 1995. Since then the state has been quietly purchasing land from willing property owners who wish to leave this untamed shore wild and rugged. The area features a rare combination of boreal forest and wetlands not found anywhere else in Door County. State fish biologists estimate that the rocky, shallow lakeshore adjacent to this site provide spawning beds for a staggering 90 percent of Lake Michigan's whitefish.

Winding north on Q, you'll be driving parallel to North Bay. North Bay is accessible by boat off North Bay Road via County ZZ at Sister Bay. This shallow, marshy bay provides a striking contrast to the limestone cliffs found on the peninsula's bayshore. Fishing for northern pike and bass is popular, but landing on the private shoreline is prohibited. County Q intersects with Highway 57 just south of Sister Bay. This busy village is the center of commerce in northern Door County, and its shops, restaurants and lodges provide a livelihood for the folks who call this part of the peninsula home.

STATE PARKS

Whitefish Dunes State Park

The entrance is well marked north of Sturgeon Bay off Highway 57. The address is 3701 Clark Lake Rd., Sturgeon Bay, WI 54235; phone: 920-823-2400.

FACILITIES:

Whitefish Dunes is a day-use park, and no camping is allowed. There are pit toilets, picnic areas, hiking trails and an excellent sand beach. A state park vehicle admission sticker is required. These are available annually or daily, and nonresidents pay more than Wisconsin residents.

RECREATION:

The park is open year-round and offers an observation deck, hiking, swimming, picnicking and cross-country skiing

The southern shore of Whitefish Dunes State Park stretches in a gentle arc of sand beach with a backdrop of dunes before giving way to rocky cliffs at Cave Point. Visitors perched on the edge of Cave Point can feel the power of Lake Michigan when the winds whip up large waves which crash against lakeshore cliffs unleashing a thunderous roar and throwing a shower of spray many feet into the air. Cave Point is preserved as a Door County Park, sandwiched between the state property which makes up Whitefish Dunes State Park today.

The swimming beach at Whitefish Dunes State Park is paradise with a lakeside view. For many years hordes of summer sun worshippers flocked to this beach to work on their tans. Before you break out your beach blanket, however, be advised that near-record high Lake Michigan water levels closed this spectacular beach in 1985–86 and again in 1997 and 1998. The closure was necessary to protect the largest sand dunes on this side of Lake Michigan while preserving the fragile community of plants which stabilize them.

If the beach is closed, take solace in the fact that

DUNES VEGETATION
Whitefish Dunes hosts a variety of plant communities because of its unique environment. A boreal forest climate is found along the lakeshore while near-desert conditions exist behind the dunes.

Whitefish Dunes State Park offers much more than sun and fun. Slip on your sneakers or lace up your hiking boots and saunter amid the largest sand dunes in Wisconsin. Well-developed hiking trails wind through woodlands and wetlands, even climbing a planked boardwalk to give you an up-close look at 93-foot-high "Old Baldy," the highest mountain of sand in Wisconsin. Wood and rope planks ease the strain of climbing "Old

WHITEFISH DUNES
STATE PARK

Baldy" while protecting the delicate and endangered plant species which cling to it. Hikers are asked to remain on the trails, respecting this fragile environment.

The ancient sand dunes found here trace their beginning to the glacial ages when a minor "dent" in the Door Peninsula shoreline became the basin of Clark Lake and Whitefish Bay. Over time lake action built up a barrier separating Clark Lake from the bay. Wind action then took over, building the dunes higher and moving them gradually farther inland. Plant life eventually stabilized some of the dunes, while others are still considered unstabilized. The stabilized dunes provide a delicate home for plant colonies attempting to eke out an existence in this harsh environment.

Whitefish Dunes has long been known for its outstanding scenic shoreline. The site was first recommended as parkland in 1937 by noted landscape architect and naturalist Jens Jensen and in 1959 the National Park Service heralded Whitefish Bay as the number one site along Wisconsin's Lake Michigan shore for park purposes.

It wasn't until 1967 that the state park received the support of Door County residents by a slim 331 votes. Much of the opposition came from summer cottage owners on adjacent Clark Lake. These vacationers were concerned about increased traffic on the lake and it was agreed the state would not encourage access to Clark Lake by developing a boat launch. Canoeists wishing to paddle this 868-acre lake now have access via a town boat launch located off Clark Lake Road. Much of Clark Lake's shoreline is developed but about 2,500 feet of shoreline remains preserved as state parkland. Fishermen will find walleye, northern pike and smallmouth bass in this 25-foot-deep lake, the deepest inland lake in Door County. Clark Lake is drained into Lake Michigan by one-mile-long Whitefish Bay Creek. This scenic creek is one of only a handful of Lake Michigan tributaries in Wisconsin where rainbow trout naturally reproduce. A spring run of rainbow followed by northern pike, suckers and smelt attract fishermen in April and May who access the creek either through the park or from a bridge located on Cave Point Road.

The varied fishery of both Clark Lake and nearby Lake Michigan has attracted cultures to this area since at least A.D. 300. An archaeological dig of a 2-acre site at the park has revealed at least eight separate cultures have occupied this area since the sand dunes began forming 3,000 years ago. The most significant of these occupations occurred around A.D. 800-900 when the Late Woodland people used this site as their seasonal home from spring through late fall harvesting whitefish and lake trout. After the fishing season drew to a close, it is believed family groups traveled to winter hunting camps along the Green Bay shoreline.

The site was discovered in the mid-1980s when the park was planning to build an interpretive center. Those plans had to be changed when Archaeologist Victoria Dirst discovered small pieces of pottery and tools in the area. In 1991 The Whitefish Bay View Site was named to the National Register of Historic Places.

The first permanent white settler of the present-day Township of Sevastopol was John Clark, who settled in the vicinity of the lake which bears his name in 1838. Commercial fishing and logging flourished at Whitefish Bay. The northern portion of the park was selectively logged in the 1920s and the Algoma Lumber Company planted red pine in the 1960s on a portion of the property they owned in the western section of the park.

Today you'll find hiking trails which snake through wetlands and slither beneath a canopy of shady sugar maples. Despite the many attractions to this varied preserve, the park's sand dunes and the rare plants which anchor them in place remain the most important feature of Whitefish Dunes. Damage to these dunes remains visible on the west side of Old Baldy, dating back to days when off-road vehicles illegally climbed these mountains of sand creating ruts which are only now beginning to support life in this harsh yet frail environment.

HIKING TRAILS

The **red trail** (2.8 miles) is a five-star trail that offers hikers an excellent example of everything Dunes State

Park has to offer. Beginning at the parking area you'll first wind through a forest in the shadow of the magnificent sand dunes that separate the red trail from Lake Michigan. The trail then provides access to Lake Michigan beach, but those who continue will reach Old Baldy, at 93 feet the tallest dune in the park. An observation deck on Old Baldy provides an unbeatable view of Lake Michigan and, on a clear day, Clark Lake as well.

The **green trail** (1.8 miles) follows the forested base of an old dune where hikers can wonder how a forest could sprout from this sandy soil. Winding back through a lowland area, walkers will wander through hemlock and white pine before returning through a beech-maple forest.

At just over four miles, the **yellow trail** is the longest trail in the park, and hikers have a chance to enjoy the green trail before the yellow trail branches off for those wishing to continue. The terrain on the yellow trail changes to an almost desert-like area before returning through a cool red pine plantation and wooded dunes.

First-time visitors will not want to miss the **white trail** (2.5-miles) since it leads to Cave Point County Park. Here, visitors can often witness Lake Michigan pounding the limestone cliffs in a thunderous roar. A spur trail shortens this loop for those on a tight schedule.

The **Brachiopod trail** is a recent addition to Whitefish Dunes. This 1.5-mile-long trail connects the White and Green trails passing through hardwood forest and an interesting bridged wetland. A brochure available in the park interpretive center explains the sixteen stations along the route. It begins at the fossil rock wall in the picnic area.

WINTER TRAILS

Cross-country skiers, snowshoers and hikers also use the 14.5 miles of trail that wind through the park. Winter storms often deposit generous snowfall on

Whitefish Dunes State Park thanks to the influence of Lake Michigan on this shoreline preserve. Skiers searching for early-season snow may encounter bare fields until arriving at this park where trails with adequate snow cover can sometimes be found. You can check first by calling 920-823-2400.

The red, green and yellow trails are groomed and can only be used for diagonal skiing. The white trail, the Brachiopod Interpretive trail and the beach area are left ungroomed and available for winter hiking, snowshoeing or skiing.

All of the winter trails begin at the greeting center and most cater to beginners. Sections of the yellow, red and green trails merit a more difficult rating as skiers return to the parking lot, but there is nothing too challenging to contend with.

Newport State Park

The entrance is five miles east of Ellison Bay off Highway 42 and is well marked. The address: 475 S. Newport Lane, Ellison Bay, WI 54210; phone: 920-854-2500.

FACILITIES:

This year-round park offers 16 backpacking campsites and one group campsite. There is no vehicle access to campsites. There are pit toilets and a central water supply. Reservations are recommended, especially during June, July and August. Thirteen of the park's 16 campsites are reservable. Campsites 3, 6, and 15 are available on a first come, first serve basis. Reservations had been available by mail but the reservation system at Wisconsin State Parks is subject to change so it's best to call the park for the latest information. A state park vehicle admission sticker is required to park at Newport. Both annual and day stickers are available and nonresidents pay more than Wisconsin residents. 2,400 acres.

RECREATION:

Places and facilities for hiking, swimming, sea kayaking, canoeing, cross-country skiing and picnicking are provided.

Wild, rugged, peaceful and inspiring, Newport State Park beckons. Visitors planning to spend the night will have to hoist a pack or pull a paddle to reach their campsite. No motor vehicles are allowed off the paved road and camping is restricted to hike-in sites. The wilderness atmosphere makes Newport unique.

Hikers will delight in the 28 miles of marked trails that wind through the woods and snake along seven miles of spectacular Lake Michigan shoreline. Sea kayakers will find sandy beaches on which to launch

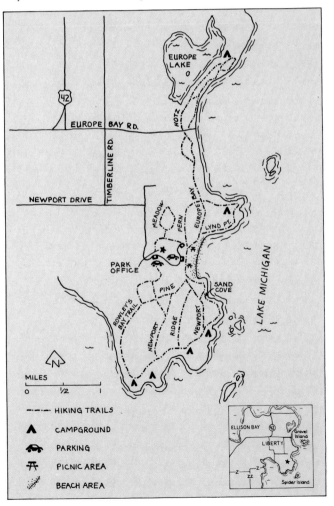

NEWPORT
STATE PARK

SNOWMOBILES PROHIBITED

Snowmobiles are outlawed from Newport State Park, but there are excellent cross-country ski trails and opportunities for snowshoeing.

Newport State Park is characterized by such tree species as sugar maple, beech, hemlock and yellow birch. Nearly the entire park has been logged in the past and the large population of white birch suggests a history of fire. The second-growth hardwood forest has returned nicely, providing an outstanding forest canopy.

and land, and canoeists have campsite access to one of the most beautiful inland lakes on the Door Peninsula.

Day visitors will relish the 3,000-foot-long sand beach, and families will enjoy picnicking along the scenic shore. Crowds are rarely a problem at Newport, and swimmers willing to hike the shoreline are certain to find plenty of room to spread out their beach blankets.

Camping at Newport State Park is a four-season affair. As summer gives way to autumn, hunters search for white-tailed deer during Wisconsin's gun deer season. Winter brings its own special magic to campers willing to stretch out on a blanket of snow. Spring makes a slow arrival on the peninsula; visitors enjoy the sense of renewal even though the trails may be soggy.

Campers must stay at designated campsites where they'll find fire rings, pit toilets and marked tent pads. Camp stoves are recommended. The 16 campsites are all accessible by foot with the closest about one mile from the parking area. The 2 campsites on Europe Lake are accessible by canoe as well as by foot, but you can't park overnight at the Europe Lake boat launch. Someone will have to hike out and move the car to the state park parking area. Paddlers willing to brave the unpredictable weather and waves of Lake Michigan have access to all of Newport's shoreline campsites by canoe or kayak. Canoeists should use extreme caution, leaving the beach only under favorable skies and a promising forecast, and should have an alternate plan for getting out if conditions turn nasty.

History buffs will enjoy searching for signs of Newport's early settlement. In the 1880s Newport was a thriving town. Settled in the 1870s by logger Hans Johnson, the community bustled with a general store, post office, dock and sawmill. When the majestic white pine trees fell to the ax, the logging jobs disappeared with them. Plans to develop streets were scrapped, and in 1919, as Newport floundered, the land was sold to Chicago investor Ferdinand Hotz.

"Without the slightest doubt the most outstanding state park possibility along the Lake Michigan shore."

So reads the reference to Door County's Newport area in a 1946 study by the Wisconsin Planning Board and the Wisconsin Conservation Department. But even following such a glowing description, it was not until September 24, 1964, that a state park became a reality. The park was named "Europe Bay State Park" because original studies had recommended inclusion of acreage on Lake Michigan's Europe Bay and inland Europe Lake. When these plans went temporarily awry, a name change to Newport State Park was deemed appropriate. When the state of Wisconsin purchased the Hotz property, it gradually removed what few buildings remained. Today, observant visitors can find the outlines of the post office in the beach area as lilac bushes and grapevines claim the hopes and dreams of a bygone era.

Thankfully, plans to include acreage on both Europe Bay and Europe Lake were not easily forgotten. In 1978, the state acquired a magnificent wooded isthmus separating Europe Lake from Lake Michigan. Known as the Hotz tract, the 170-acre parcel included a cabin that has since been removed, leaving only memories of a pioneer's past. With 28 miles of marked hiking trails and 16 backpack campsites, Newport State Park is the most popular destination for backpackers on the peninsula. The terrain is wild and rugged to behold, but gentle and mellow to hike.

TEMPERATURE
The average high temperature for Newport in July is a balmy 80 degrees but the low drops down to 57. During January, high temp is 27 degrees, the low a chilly 10.

HIKING TRAILS

Newport Trail: This trail is the longest (4.5 miles), widest and most used trail in the park. Easily hiked in three hours, the trail forms a loop along old logging roads still used for park maintenance. Beginning from either beach parking lot, hikers will wind through low-lying areas thick with white cedar, balsam fir and hemlock. Keep a lookout for the huge virgin white pines near the intersection with the Sand Cove Trail, and you'll have an idea of how this area looked during the last century.

Europe Bay Trail: Beginning at parking lot 3, the Europe

Bay Trail (3.25 miles) heads north along an old logging trail through maple and beech forests to Europe Bay. Past the Fern Trail junction, ancient sand ridges run parallel to the beach. Between the ridges water has been trapped, forming tiny, delicate bog communities. These ridges are former shores of a receding glacial lake. Just to the east of the trail is Europe Bay with a 1.5-mile-long sand beach that provides a panorama that includes Lake Michigan, Death's Door Passage and Plum and Detroit islands.

Hotz Trail: The varied terrain makes this two-mile trail a park favorite. The trail begins on the north side of Europe Bay Road (accessible off Europe Bay Trail) and passes through a forest of red pine, oak and beech trees. As you climb the sand ridge you will see Europe Lake on your left. It is believed this lake was a bay of Lake Michigan until wave action deposited sand that today forms the ridge separating the two bodies of water. Over a mile of the eastern shore of this 274-acre lake is part of Newport State Park. As you continue down the trail you'll find several points where both Europe Lake and Lake Michigan are visible. Your return trip takes you to the Lake Michigan shore, adding to the beauty and variety of this glorious hike.

Lynd Point Trail: This two-mile trail provides access to campsites 1 and 2 off the Europe Bay Trail while taking hikers along the rocky Lake Michigan shoreline. The tiny island to the northeast of Lynd Point is Gravel Island National Wildlife Refuge, home to nesting gulls, cormorants and shorebirds.

Fern Trail: The short (.75 mile) Fern Trail begins at lot 3 near the picnic area and winds through an old spruce plantation. Be on the lookout for wildflowers in the spring and summer.

Monarch Trail: This trail (2 miles) is Newport's self-guided nature trail. Beginning at the visitor contact station near the park entrance, the loop includes 36 trail stations to help you identify trees, flowers and wildlife.

SUNSHINE
The odds of encountering sunshine favor campers at Newport from May through September. In November and December sunshine averages only 40%, and the remaining months, somewhere in between.

(opposite page)
Serenity can be found at Newport State Park.

143

Upland Trail: This loop (2 miles) provides park visitors the best opportunity to spot white-tailed deer grazing in the open areas at dusk. Reached from the visitor's station near the park entrance, this loop circles through a 50-year-old spruce plantation, hidden meadows and forest.

Rowley's Bay Trail: The 2.5-mile Rowley's Bay Trail connects the Pine Trail with campsites at Varney's Point. The trail leads through meadows and fields that are slowly being reclaimed by the forest after being cleared for crops.

Sand Cove Trail: This is a short (1 mile) track that cuts off of the Newport Trail and follows the lakeshore to Sand Cove, a beautiful, secluded sand beach that beckons overheated hikers to take a swim.

CROSS-COUNTRY SKI TRAILS

These hiking trails are recombined to become longer Nordic trails in the winter. Generally they are flat, easy and forgiving even for beginners, but northern portions of the white trail near Europe Lake lead to an exhilarating, albeit brief, hill to be avoided by rookies. Snow cover is best from December to mid-March, but if in doubt, call first: 920-854-2500. Even if snowfall is poor, pac boots will provide for a pleasant hike in this year-round wonderland.

The **white trail** (7 miles) begins at parking lot 3. Start on the yellow trail before joining the white loop as you head toward Europe Lake. This trail follows the path of an old logging road through maple and beech forest. It is the longest single trail in the park, and offers great views of both frozen Europe Lake and icy cold Lake Michigan. An alternative starting point is reached off Europe Bay Road with access to the ski trail just west of Europe Bay Town Park.

Also from parking lot 3, the **red loop** (5 miles) winds through a forest of white cedar, balsam fir, hemlock and white pine. The trail follows an old logging road that becomes the main thoroughfare for hikers during the summer months. The going is easy and the trail is pleasant, forming an easy connection to the blue loop for an extended journey.

You can pick up the **blue loop** (5 miles) from parking lot 1. This picturesque loop takes skiers along the shores of Lake Michigan through a cedar forest before reaching Varney's Point. The wind often whips along this stretch of shoreline and the trail can become icy during periods of freeze and thaw.

The short **orange trail** (2 miles), accessible from lot 1 only, takes skiers along the park's self-guided nature trail. The loop winds through cedar swamp and hardwood forest before returning to the parking lot.

The **yellow trail** (1 mile) is a nice loop for beginners. As the trail circles through an old spruce plantation, novices will get a feel for the natural beauty of the park and the serenity of Nordic skiing.

TOWN, VILLAGE AND COUNTY PARKS

Cave Point County Park (18.6 acres)

Cave Point County Park is well known for its wave-worn limestone ledges, underwater caves and stirring view of Lake Michigan. When the waves of Lake Michigan are crashing against the caves, water erupts from the limestone cliffs in a thunderous roar, creating a magnificent scene. Fishermen, skilled scuba divers, experienced sea kayakers, photography buffs, and nature observers find the park a great delight. Facilities include picnic tables, fire rings and parking for about 20 cars. Whitefish Dunes State Park borders this preserve on three sides.

Schauer Town Park (1.5 acres)

Schauer Town Park is located just north of Whitefish Dunes State Park and provides public boat access to Lake Michigan with a one-lane boat ramp. There is parking for about eight cars with trailers.

Lakeside Town Park (3.3 acres)

Located off Highway 57, in the heart of Jacksonport, Lakeside Town Park provides a pleasant sand swimming beach and a large grassy lawn on which to relax. This park is the center of activity during the annual Maifest celebration held each May. Playground equipment, grills and parking facilities are available. Attempts to maintain the boat launch ramp have been generally unsatisfactory because shifting sand continues to cover the ramp.

Jacksonport Community Town Park (10 acres)

Located west of the village center, the Jacksonport Community Town Park provides a lighted softball field and a pair of tennis courts. The grounds house the town hall and the fire station as well. This is a pleasant site to take in a baseball game when players from the Door County summer baseball league step up to bat.

POTAWATOMI VILLAGE

The Potawatomi Indians had a large village known as "Mechingin" in the vicinity of the present-day village of Jacksonport.

146

Meridian County Park (92 acres)

Meridian County Park is the second-largest county park in the Door County park system. A wayside on Highway 57 provides access to this undeveloped preserve, but its rugged nature makes exploration difficult. The wayside is maintained by the State Department of Transportation and includes restrooms and picnic facilities. This heavily wooded park is wet and marshy, providing excellent wildlife habitat. An old logging road through the property has been converted to a snowmobile trail. This park is adjacent to the Lyle Harter-Matter Sanctuary.

Lyle Harter-Matter Sanctuary
County Park (40 acres)

Donated to Door County in 1945 as a sanctuary, this 40-acre tract contiguous to Meridian County Park is completely undeveloped. This preserve is not served by a road. A magnificent high sand dune runs through the preserve, and a beautiful forest canopy of both deciduous and coniferous species covers most of the property. A marsh is also found on the preserve, creating an excellent undisturbed habitat for wildlife.

Baileys Harbor Recreation Field (27 acres)

The Baileys Harbor Recreation Field is noted for its fine baseball diamond, complete with fencing, bleachers, batter's cage and concession stand.

Anclam Town Park (1 acre)

Centrally located in Baileys Harbor, adjacent to Highway 57, Anclam Park provides a sand swimming beach and a one-lane boat ramp providing access to Lake Michigan. A protective breakwater juts into the lake. Playground equipment, picnic tables and a grill are provided for those wishing to enjoy a picnic.

Baileys Harbor Fire Station Field (1.6 acres)

Located adjacent to the fire station in Baileys Harbor, this park offers a pair of blacktop tennis courts, a grass field and parking for about one dozen cars.

Baileys Harbor Ridges County Park (30 acres)

This park is famous for its two rangelight houses, used to provide a line of sight for mariners entering Baileys Harbor in bygone days. The houses still stand, but the original lights have been removed and modern directional rangelights have been installed elsewhere on the property by the Coast Guard. The rangelights are considered historical landmarks. A fine sand beach is located on the harbor side of Ridges Drive and is popular for both swimming and sunning. A parking lot has ample room for those using the beach or hiking along trails that lead to the adjacent Ridges Sanctuary. In 1972, Door County officials leased the property north of Ridges Drive to the Ridges Sanctuary. This group now maintains the property and the rangelight houses.

Boes Town Park (.15 acre)

This small park provides boat access to Moonlight Bay, offering a launch ramp with a removable pier. The site is small but pleasantly wooded. Parking is available for only two cars, so if you're planning an outing on Moonlight Bay, plan on arriving early.

Town of Liberty Grove School Forest (60 acres)

The 60-acre Town of Liberty Grove Plantation Forest is located southwest of Sister Bay off Old Stage Road. This unmarked woodlot is publicly owned but difficult to explore because its boundaries are not defined. It is, however, a welcome tract of green space and it is comforting to know it will remain a visual oasis for travelers and a permanent refuge for plants and wildlife.

Sand Bay Town Park (4 acres)

An excellent sand beach and a beautiful view of Spider Island and Newport State Park characterize Sand Bay Town Park. Located at the intersection of Sand Bay Road and Water's End Road, this secluded beach has a wooded shore and parking for about six or seven cars. Picnic tables and grills are provided. This park provides an excellent free public launch to kayakers wishing to explore the Mink River Estuary. After launching, paddle

(opposite page)
A woodland garden blankets the forest floor.

north, past Rowley's Bay, about one-half mile to the mouth of this Nature Conservancy preserve.

Europe Bay Town Park (2 acres)

This secluded sand beach is surrounded by Newport State Park and provides convenient access to one of the finest stretches of white sand on the peninsula. A gravel road leads to the beach. Watch for the small sign as you make the final turn into Newport State Park. The pleasantly wooded grounds here are perfect for a picnic, and the beach provides an excellent launch site for kayakers.

PRESERVES

Kangaroo Lake

From Highway 57 one mile south of Baileys Harbor take County Highway E west approximately one mile to the causeway separating Kangaroo Lake. Park and put-in on the northern side of the causeway. Hiking access: Continue on County E over the causeway until the highway takes a sharp right. Proceed right one-quarter mile to the small primitive parking area on the right-hand side of the road.

FACILITIES:
Open year-round with hiking and canoe access.

RECREATION:
Canoeing, hiking, bird-watching, fishing, snow-shoeing.
A chorus of frogs and the flapping wings of a woodcock mark the arrival of spring along the northern shores of Kangaroo Lake just southeast of Baileys Harbor.
This 1,100-acre lake takes its name from its unique "kangaroo" shape. A paved causeway built before the turn of the century supports County Highway E and separates the undeveloped northern "head" of the lake

from the development that has occurred along the southern reaches of Door County's largest inland lake.

Door County locals have long appreciated Kangaroo Lake for its clear water, inland fishing opportunities and scenic value. Now the Nature Conservancy is celebrating its biological richness as well.

An extensive marsh surrounds the northern shore of Kangaroo Lake before gradually surrendering to a limestone plateau west of the lake. This forested plateau rises 110 feet above the lake's surface providing a striking alternative to the marshland below.

KANGAROO LAKE

According to the Conservancy, Piel Creek, which feeds the lake, is one of fewer than fifteen sites in the world where the federally endangered Hines emerald dragonfly has been located. Noted for its 3.3-inch-long wingspan, this 2.5-inch-long emerald green insect is typically found in wetlands overlying dolomite bedrock. This area is one of only two known breeding sites in the United States where this dragonfly survives.

In 1995, the Nature Conservervancy, in cooperation with the Door County Land Trustees and the Kangaroo Lake Association, acquired 117 acres along the northwestern shore of the lake. This parcel is accessible by foot, but a canoe provides the most interesting perspective. Paddling along the shore canoeists may encounter black terns which nest in the marsh or spot ospreys or bald eagles soaring overhead.

Hikers will travel through birch, white cedar and black ash forest while making their way to lakeshore along a series of primitive unmarked trails. Despite the lack of trail signage, visitors will have little trouble navigating the route to the shore, but be sure to remain on Conservancy property as you enjoy the riches of Kangaroo Lake.

Shivering Sands

Black bears have been known to take refuge amid the shallow lakes and forested sand dunes within Lake Michigan's Shivering Sands wetland complex north of Sturgeon Bay.

The area takes its name from the creek which drains Dunes Lake into Lake Michigan. It is here the sand dunes bordering the tiny stream are said to quiver or "shiver" in the wind.

Located off scenic Glidden Drive, the Shivering Sands complex incorporates three privately owned lakes and several springs amid a lowland conifer forest.

This area is likely the largest undeveloped privately owned roadless area in Door County. It encompasses a staggering 3,400 acres and may be the largest contiguous cedar swamp in Wisconsin according to the Nature Conservancy.

Dunes, Shawartz and Arbter are the three shallow wetland lakes which make up this nationally significant complex. They are surrounded by cattails ringed with white cedar and tamarack. Dunes Lake at 81 acres is the largest of the three lakes. It is fed by Donlan's Creek which provides the only possible public access by canoe or kayak since the property surrounding the lake is privately owned by a Door County-based hunting club.

The Nature Conservancy first took an interest in the property in 1984 when its staff took bird and plant inventories. What it found was impressive. Rare dwarf lake iris bloom in the upland forest while sandhill cranes breed on Dunes Lake. Spring peepers fill the April air with song and otters frolic within the inland lakes.

To date, the Nature Conservancy has ownership of 192 acres of lowland cedar swamp and forested sand dunes. Special access to the Nature Conservancy property is available only for educational or research purposes by contacting the Wisconsin Chapter office at 633 West Main Street, Madison, WI 53703 or calling 608-251-8140.

Depending on water levels, paddlers may be able to slip a canoe or kayak in Donlan's Creek where it crosses Haberli Road north of the complex and paddle one mile south to Dunes Lake. Landing on Dunes Lake is prohibited and anyone visiting this unique area must use the utmost care to ensure its continued protection.

Mink River Estuary

The preserve is on Rowley's Bay, southeast of Ellison Bay. Exit Highway 42 north of Ellison Bay at County NP (Newport Drive) and watch for the Nature Conservancy marker as the road takes a sharp left. Also accessible from Ellison Bay by taking Mink River Road, which takes you to the southern part of the preserve. From Sister Bay take Highway 42 north to County Z and turn right. Follow County Z to Mink River Road.

FACILITIES:

A day-use area, the preserve is open year-round for observation by foot or canoe.

RECREATION:

Canoeing, sea kayaking, bird-watching, fishing and hiking.

MINK RIVER SANCTUARY

SEICHES

Seiches are the local fluctuations in Lake Michigan's water level caused by blowing wind. In the Mink River the seiches cause the lake and water level to mix, which creates a rare fresh water estuary.

154

The Mink River is one of the Door Peninsula's geographic wonders. Paddlers viewing this ancient wetland for the first time can turn back the hands of time to an era of wild shores and dark forests.

Fed by alkaline springs, the Mink River meets Lake Michigan at Rowley's Bay creating a rich freshwater estuary on the northeastern shore of the peninsula. An estuary is an area at the mouth of a river where the current meets the tide.

ROWLEY'S BAY
Rowley's Bay is noted for its excellent smallmouth bass fishing. It also provides boaters access to the Mink River.

Although most estuaries have been destroyed by development or pollution, the Mink River has remained largely undisturbed. In 1976 the Nature Conservancy recognized the irreplaceable value of the Mink and began efforts to acquire its surrounding shore. To date, this private conservation organization has protected 150,000 acres of Mink River shoreland through acquisition and conservation easements.

The Mink River is a critical spawning area for fish and an important nesting and resting place for both resident and migrating birds. In all, the Nature Conservancy estimates that over 200 bird species may pass through the area annually including the Cooper's hawk, a threatened species in Wisconsin. Paddlers enjoying the river are asked to avoid sliding their boats through the marsh grass at the headwaters of the Mink from May through July to protect nesting waterfowl. Other wildlife including beaver, muskrat and white-tailed deer make their home in this unique wetland which is open to hunting during November, January and February. A wide variety of fish find sanctuary from predators along the river's shallow shore while waterfowl feed on the wild rice which stretches from the river bed.

Summer visitors to the Mink River often arrive by canoe or sea kayak but exploration is also possible on foot. There are walk-in areas on each side of the river but the eastern shore remains the most accessible since trails on the western side of the river can be confusing to follow.

A trailhead is located off County NP (Newport Drive) just east of Ellison Bay via Highway 42. From here, the one-half-mile-long Hemlock Trail meanders through the upland cedar and hemlock forest to a pleasant picnic site on the banks of the river. As you approach the landing you'll find the uplands gradually giving way to lowland cedar, and as you near the river, marshland prevails. Two plant species threatened with extinction in Wisconsin grow wild here: the dune thistle and the dwarf lake iris. Bulrush, a marsh plant found in abundance here, serves to protect the inland plant communities by withstanding the constant wave and current action caused by Lake Michigan.

The landing is a fine place to keep a lookout for the bald eagles, ospreys or sandhill cranes known to visit the estuary. It is also a wonderful site to contemplate what peninsula pioneers once suspected: That the Mink River was subject to tides. Researchers have since confirmed what early pioneers long suspected: that the three-mile-long Mink River does in fact flow in both directions. Using sophisticated water-level recorders, researchers have concluded that the water level in the Mink rises and falls as lake water flows in and then out of the river approximately every hour.

Archaeologists report that American Indians were drawn to the area over 2,000 years ago and two village sites have been identified.

In the late 1800s booms of logs where floated down the Mink to ships awaiting them on Rowley's Bay. Today, the log booms are gone and visitors to the Mink River Estuary will find this ecosystem is much the same as when Potawatomi Indians inhabited this region more than a century ago. The Nature Conservancy is working to ensure Mink River remains an ancient escape for twentieth-century visitors.

Ridges Sanctuary

Take Highway 57 north of Baileys Harbor to County Q.

FACILITIES:

The Ridges Sanctuary is a year-round facility offering hiking trails, a nature center and an observation platform.

156

RECREATION:

Guided nature hikes, bird-watching and hiking.

The Ridges Sanctuary is an outstanding natural classroom. This private nature preserve was established in 1937 by visionary conservationists "concerned for the future of the botanically rich area lying between Baileys Harbor and Moonlight Bay," according to the sanctuary trail guide. Time seems to be measured not in minutes and hours at the Ridges Sanctuary, but rather in eons and epochs. The trails follow some of the 17 ancient sand dune ridges formed as Lake Michigan advanced and retreated through the ages.

In 1936 plans were under way to build a trailer park here. With the advent of modern navigational techniques, the federal government had no more use for the 40-acre rangelight preserve that provided a line of sight to guide ships into Baileys Harbor. The land was deeded to the county for the park.

Local conservationists Jens Jenson and Emma Toft led the fight to preserve the ridges. Local legend has it that "Miss Emma" threw herself in front of a bulldozer to stop the trailer park, but in fact the battle was won through persuasion and reason as Toft convinced the county to turn the land over to the Ridges Sanctuary group. The original 40 acres has grown into a 910-acre wildflower preserve with some 2,800 members supporting it. Today the public is welcome even though the sanctuary receives no tax dollars and purchases its own land for preservation. The sanctuary has the additional status of being recognized today as a national natural landmark by the Department of the Interior.

Most travelers time their visits to coincide with one of the May-to-October tours guided by sanctuary naturalists. Many are drawn by the 28 species of native orchids found growing in this botanical wonderland. Early June is the best time to see the Ridges Sanctuary's dwarf iris, gay wings and arctic primrose in bloom. Late June finds the orchids in bloom. In addition to the wide variety of wildflowers growing here, over a dozen plant species on Wisconsin's endangered and threatened list call the sanctuary home. A self-guided tour is available

RIDGES RANGELIGHTS

A lighthouse was built on Baileys Harbor in 1852, but in 1870 it was replaced by two separate, sychronized beacons known as rangelights. These lights once consisted of kerosene lanterns magnified by thick lenses. They have been restored, but are no longer in service.

for the independent visitor, but those venturing on the trails are asked not to pick the flowers or disturb the wildlife.

Toft Point Nature Conservancy

From Baileys Harbor turn right on Ridge Road at the north end of the village. Just over the small creek, turn left on the small, unmarked one-lane road. There is room for only a few cars at the gate. In winter, park on Ridge Road (if possible) and ski down the small town road to the lakeshore.

FACILITIES:

Hiking and cross-country ski trails are open year-round.

RECREATION:

The conservancy is open to the public for passive recreation including bird-watching, nature hikes and skiing.

An unspoiled tract of virgin timber and untamed shoreline awaits visitors to Toft Point on Moonlight Bay. Thanks to the Nature Conservancy and the remarkable Emma Toft, the deep, dark and intriguing forest that "Miss Emma" cherished shall remain wild forever.

Adjacent to Ridges Sanctuary, the original 275-acre Toft Point Natural Area was acquired by the Nature Conservancy in two separate tracts beginning in 1976. The acquisition was contingent on the stipulation that Miss Toft be allowed to remain in her "Mud Bay" home, as she called it, as long as she was willing and able. Those who knew Miss Emma tell tales of her scolding hikers audacious enough to pick flowers growing wild on the adjacent Ridges Sanctuary. "Sir," she was heard to say, "if you pick all these flowers there'll be none for others to enjoy." In 1982, the feisty guardian of Moonlight Bay died at age 91, bequeathing to all the natural treasure she had fought to preserve.

Expansion of the Toft Point Natural Area was

(opposite page)

Tamaracks and reed grasses border low-lying swales at the Ridges Sanctuary, a world-famous wildflower preserve.

159

MOONLIGHT BAY
Moonlight Bay is
popular among perch,
bass and pike fishermen.
An inlet here provides
canoe access to Mud
Lake.

accomplished in 1976. A 325-acre contiguous tract was purchased by the Nature Conservancy from the Ajax Lumber Company and the Lighthouse Point Development Corporation. The preserve now encompasses 633 acres, including 2.5 miles of wild Lake Michigan shoreline on Moonlight Bay. The preserve has been turned over to the University of Wisconsin-Green Bay and today serves as a research site and a natural classroom, as well as being open to the public for passive recreation.

Mud Lake Wildlife Area

From Baileys Harbor, take Highway 57 north to County Q. Turn right (east) and take County Q 2.5 miles to Reibolt's Creek, then canoe one mile upstream to Mud Lake. Or, just across Reibolt's Creek, follow Sunrise Road north 1.2 miles, then park and hike down the road to the unimproved landing on Mud Lake.

FACILITIES:
    The wildlife area is open year-round with canoe access.

RECREATION:
    Hiking, canoeing, bird-watching, hunting (in season) and cross-country skiing.
    Mud Lake Wildlife Area is an outstanding resource characterized by its remote setting and peaceful, undis- turbed atmosphere.
    The lake itself is a shallow 155-acre drainage sur- rounded by extensive second-growth white cedar swamp. Canoeing provides the best access to the area, but many visitors hike in as well. Drained by Reibolt's Creek, Mud Lake provides one of the few remaining natural waterfowl production areas on the Door Peninsula.
    The large size and remote character of this natural area provide habitat for species requiring large tracts of undisturbed wilderness including black bear, coyote and bobcat. Visitors may also encounter white-tailed

RIDGES
SANCTUARY,
TOFT POINT,
MUD LAKE

MUD
LAKE

WALK-IN
SITE

REIBOLTS CREEK

SUNSET DRIVE

Q

MOONLIGHT BAY

MARSH AREA

HIKING
TRAIL

MARSH

57

Q

RIDGES DR.

BAILEYS HARBOR

POINT DR.

N

MILES

0   ¼   ½   ¾   1

⬡   ENTRANCES

⬗   CANOE LAUNCH

▒   RIDGES SANCTUARY

▨   TOFT POINT NATURE CONSERVANCY

▧   MUD LAKE WILDLIFE AREA

MUD
LAKE

57

Q

BAILEYS HARBOR

deer standing chest-high in Reibolt's Creek, or ruffed grouse exploding from thick cover. Birdwatchers may find wood ducks, pileated woodpeckers or even an occasional sharp-shinned hawk, known to nest in the adjacent Ridges Sanctuary.

Mud Lake has a maximum depth of five feet, though most of the lake is less than three feet deep. It is about 1.35 miles long and about a half mile wide. The largest of the three unnamed streams that enter Mud Lake has its outlet in the northwest corner of the lake and is about 2.5 miles long.

The state of Wisconsin began acquiring property for the Mud Lake Wildlife Area in 1966. The major landholder was Leeland Thorp, who owned 1,040 acres surrounding the lake and wished it preserved as a wildlife habitat. Since then, over 1,000 acres of the preserve have been designated a state scientific area. Further, Mud Lake Wildlife Area, Ridges Sanctuary, Toft Point, Moonlight Bay Bedrock Beach and Baileys Harbor Boreal Forest in combination have been designated a national natural landmark by the Department of the Interior.

Baileys Harbor Boreal Forest and Moonlight Bay Bedrock Beach Natural Areas

Bedrock beaches alternate with complex wetlands to stand guard off Cana Cove where some 90 percent of Lake Michigan's whitefish spawn east of Baileys Harbor.

In 1991, as pressure was mounting to develop one of the last stretches of untamed Door County lakeshore, state biologists developed a plan to forever protect and preserve this critical habitat. Approved in 1995, it's called the Baileys Harbor Boreal Forest and Wetland Project. The goal of the 1,200-acre project is "to preserve, restore and maintain nationally significant coastal communities and uplands which harbor botanical features unique to the Great Lakes coastal ecosystems."

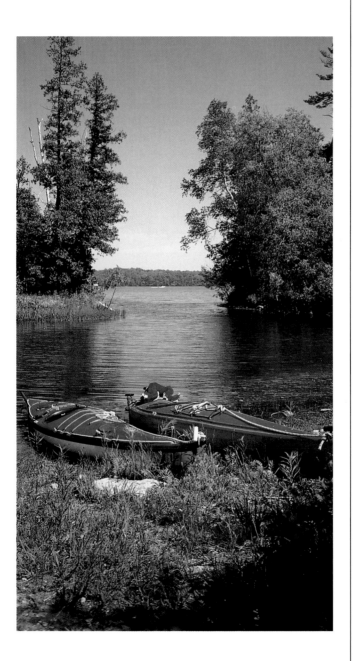

Europe Lake offers
kayakers a pleasant
day outing.

DUNE BUILDING

Vast amounts of sand erodes from the shoreline and dunes during Lake Michigan's high-water periods. As the waters recede, the expanse of beach increases and the fine sand particles are exposed to the wind, beginning anew the process of dune-building.

(opposite page)

Chasing those lakeshore waves at Ridges County Park in Baileys Harbor.

Today sea kayakers exploring the rocky shelves between North Bay and Cana Island will find a rich boreal forest and wetland dominated by white spruce and balsam fir giving way to cobble and bedrock beaches.

The cool moist climate of the lakeshore coupled with the ever-changing water levels of Lake Michigan create a micro climate which harbors at least 59 rare plant species. These plants include the bird's-eye primrose and the calypso orchid along with a host of unusual insects including the Hines emerald dragonfly. Further, fisheries biologists estimate that of the 1.2 million whitefish swimming these waters, 1.1 million spawn in the coastal waters from Moonlight Bay to North Bay. Migratory shorebirds and waterfowl also rely on these shores and it is one of the few known nesting sites in Wisconsin of the common goldeneye.

Nearby, the state has also been purchasing undeveloped lakeshore parcels on Moonlight Bay for inclusion in the Moonlight Bay Bedrock Beach State Natural Area.

There are currently some 60 private property owners holding parcels within the project boundaries. The state will only purchase these in-holdings from willing sellers and acquisition is expected to be an ongoing process. To frustrate negotitations, developers have been known to tempt lakeshore landowners by tripling the offering the state has made for the same parcel. Nevertheless many conscientious landowners are resisting development and recognizing this is the last chance to save a wild shore.

Currently, a sea kayak is the best means to explore this unique part of the peninsula. Put in at the Cana Island causeway and paddle north to Cana Cove or south past Boes Point to Moonlight Bay. Exploration on foot is currently limited. Long-term plans call for a small parking area to be developed off County Q if a large enough parcel is acquired to permit foot traffic without damaging this delicate environment.

Cana Island Lighthouse

Cana Island captures the essence of Door County's rugged natural beauty and colorful maritime history.

For over 130 years the lighthouse on this small Lake Michigan island has stood witness through calm seas and ferocious storms. Light keepers once fueled the beacon with whale oil guiding sailors past the treacherous reefs and around the rugged Door County shoreline. Despite the best efforts of these keepers, the lake bottom surrounding this island remains a graveyard of lost ships and shattered dreams.

The story of the lighthouse begins in 1869 when the 89-foot-high tower and the light-keeper's dwelling were constructed here. The two-family house was built for the light keeper and his assistant and for many years two families lived beneath one roof. The keeper's logs are filled with tales of bravery and romance, hardship and struggle, rescue and loss. One account describes an awesome gale in the 1870s which sunk seven ships in the region. The keeper reported huge waves breaking over the house and spray from the breakers reaching the glass on the tower 80 feet high! Other accounts chart the peaceful history of island life where one keeper and his wife raised seven sons and competed against nearby Eagle Tower lighthouse for "best kept" awards.

The last lighthouse keepers played a different role from that of their predecessors. For over 15 years beginning in 1977, Louie and Rosie Janda lived as summer caretakers on the island hosting visitors, performing maintenance and raising five children.

Today, the light is automated and the tower is closed to the public but visitors can still step back in time to enjoy the peaceful spirit of Cana Island thanks to the efforts of the Door County Maritime Museum. The museum leases the lighthouse building from the Coast Guard and it has done much to restore the dwelling and maintain the grounds. For a small fee visitors can tour the grounds from mid-May through October with

CANA ISLAND CAUSEWAY MYSTERY

The development of Cana Island remains a mystery. Although there is much speculation the rock causeway is man-made, there is no documentation that this is the case. In fact, there is some evidence it is natural. Waves break around the island in a unique pattern and when the lake is high they meet in the area of the causeway often depositing stones upon their departure.

a museum staff member.

A move is under way to turn the island into a county park. This movement is not without controversy. Many residents are justifiably fearful the quiet setting and peaceful atmosphere could be disrupted by increased access. But Cana Island has weathered many storms in the past and there is little doubt it will survive this political storm as well.

Open 10 A.M.—5 P.M. mid-May through October, Cana Island is Door County's most accessible island. It is located off County Q on Cana Island Road east of Baileys Harbor. A stone causeway connects the island to the mainland. During periods of high water you'll get your feet wet reaching the lighthouse but it's certainly worth the effort.

CANA ISLAND LIGHTHOUSE LENS
The beacon at Cana Island Lighthouse houses the original five-foot-high Fresnel lens. This marvel of engineering depends on prisms, which surround the top and bottom of the lens, to gather light from a tiny source focusing it into an intense beam visible 18 miles away.

BEACHES

Whitefish Bay Dunes Beach

The glorious dunes at Whitefish Bay have long been a favorite haunt among local beachcombers. Near-record high water levels on Lake Michigan forced park rangers to close this beach in 1985 and 1986 and again in 1997 and 1998. The closure was necessary to protect the plant life which stabilize the sand dunes from the footsteps of visitors. If your heart is set on a day of sun and fun at the dunes be sure to first call and check on current beach conditions (920-823-2400).

The water temperature of Lake Michigan at Whitefish Dunes is usually cooler than on the bayside of the peninsula, but the sizzling sand on a hot summer day can quickly comfort shivering swimmers. When the whitecaps are breaking, there is no better beach on Door Peninsula for body surfing, but use caution. Rip currents claimed the life of a swimmer here shortly before the park staff outlawed swimming at the far end of the beach. Take Highway 57 north of Sturgeon Bay. Turn right at Whitefish Bay Road to Whitefish Dunes State Park. A vehicle admission sticker is required.

Schauer Park Beach

Bicyclists enjoying the scenic roads surrounding Whitefish Dunes State Park will find swimming opportunities adjacent to the boat ramp off Schauer Town Park. This tiny beach is no substitute for the wonderful sand of Whitefish Dunes, but when you're hot and tired it's a pleasant discovery.

Jacksonport Lakeside Beach

It's not surprising that Potawatomi Indians had a large village near Jacksonport when you consider they had a comfortable sand beach on which to camp. This beach and the surrounding park is a busy place during the annual Jacksonport Maifest celebration, but typically it's a quiet, comforting place to sun and swim.

RIP CURRENTS
When Whitefish Dunes State Park beach is open, high waves can batter the shore offering excellent body surfing opportunities. These waves can also be dangerous, since rip currents can develop, frustrating the efforts of even strong swimmers to return to shore. To guard against these conditions, rangers have instituted a "no swimming" area in the first 225 yards of the beach.

Anclam Town Beach

Easy access to the center and a great view of Baileys Harbor make the Anclam Town Beach a convenient place for a quick swim. Located off Highway 57, the beach is protected by a large breakwater that juts into Lake Michigan.

Baileys Harbor Ridges Beach

This local beach is a favorite of those wishing to beat the crowds on a hot August day. Located off County Q, a portion of this park is leased to the Ridges Sanctuary.

Sand Bay Park Beach

Not to be confused with the private resort of the same name in southern Door County, Sand Bay Beach is located just south of Rowley Bay in the northeastern corner of the county. This secluded beach is located at the intersection of Sand Bay Road and Water's End Road. It offers delightful swimming and a great view of Newport State Park and Spider island. This is also a convenient place to launch a sea kayak for exploration of the nearby Mink River.

Europe Bay Town Park Beach

Easy access, shallow water and a beautiful natural setting characterize the beach at Europe Bay Town Park. The town of Liberty Grove has managed to maintain the rustic beauty of this beach by keeping development to a minimum and resisting the temptation to pave the gravel road to this local gem. Sun worshippers looking for elbow room need only head down the beach to adjacent Newport State Park. Here you'll find peace, quiet, sand and sun with a lush green forest at your back and a sweet-water sea nipping your toes. Parking is limited here, so plan to arrive early if you hope to stake a claim.

Exit Highway 42 north of Ellison Bay at the turnoff to Newport State Park on Europe Bay Road. Follow Europe Bay Road until it turns to gravel, concluding at the beach parking area.

Europe Lake Beach

Swimmers who can't quite muster the courage to brave the chilly waters of Lake Michigan will find Europe Lake a pleasant (and warmer) alternative. When lake levels are low, a delightful beach is exposed along Europe Lake's northeast shore. This beach is part of Newport State Park, but it borders a handful of private cottages, so please respect their privacy. Access to this inland beach is best by canoe, but many parents wade the knee-deep water from the boat landing with their children on their shoulders, or with a picnic lunch in a day pack.

Exit Highway 42 north of Ellison Bay at Europe Bay Road. Turn left on Timberline Road to Europe Lake Lane and turn right (east) to the public landing at Europe Lake.

Sand Cove Beach

Sand Cove is one of those rare finds you stumble upon when you're hot, tired and ready for a dip. Located in Newport State Park, Sand Cove is often overlooked by beachcombers; who are content to remain on the more accessible Europe Bay Beach. Those willing to take the half-mile hike to find Sand Cove will find a beautiful beach that is often empty, quiet and peaceful.

From lot 2 of Newport State Park (a state park vehicle admission sticker is required), head down the Newport Trail, but keep to the far left trail when it branches off.

BICYCLE TOURS

Whitefish Dunes Bicycle Tour (10 miles)

This tour follows inland Clark Lake on heavily wooded narrow roads tailor-made for bicycle travel. Swimming opportunities are available. In addition to following the Clark Lake shoreline, it also wanders by rural farms and fields.

After exiting Whitefish Dunes State Park, turn left on

Cave Point Drive and follow this beautiful road through parkland before taking the first right on unmarked South Shore Drive. At the first intersection turn left and head for the shore, where a public swimming beach awaits you. After taking a swim or enjoying the view, a left turn from the beach will take you back to Cave

WHITEFISH DUNES
BICYCLE TOUR

Whitefish Dunes Bicycle Tour

- - - BICYCLE ROUTE (10 MILES)

Point Drive. Continue on Cave Point Drive to West
Shore Drive and turn right. Clark Lake will again be
visible. Take West Shore Drive to Townline Road and

turn left on Townline. The dead-end road here offers a small boat launch and a potential swimming location. From Townline take the first right onto Loritz Road. At sunset, deer may be seen in the fields off this road. Continue to Bagnall Road then turn right on Jorns Road (unpaved for two blocks), then cross Highway 57. Remain on Jorns Road to Cave Point Road and head back to Whitefish Dunes State Park.

Baileys Harbor Tour

This 23-mile tour winds through the Ridges Sanctuary to the historic Cana Island Lighthouse.

Beginning in downtown Baileys Harbor, head north through town to County Q. Pass Old County Q and turn right on Cana Island Road. At the first stop sign turn right, then bear left on paved roads to the Cana Island Lighthouse. A stone causeway provides foot access to Cana Island and its historic lighthouse between 10:00 A.M. and 5:00 P.M. Backtrack on Cana Island Road to County Q once again and turn right. Cross Highway 57 to Townline Road and turn left. Continue on Townline Road past German and Pioneer Roads. Once past Pioneer Road, Townline becomes Summach Road. Continue on Summach Road to the stop sign and turn right on West Meadow Road. Continue past Cedar, bearing left at the stop sign, and you'll be on County F. County F will lead you back to Baileys Harbor.

Mink River Rolling Bicycle Tour (9.5 miles)

Tour country roads through orchards, rolling farmland and small woodlots in the town of Liberty Grove while following the path of the Mink River. The terrain is gentle, and although you won't see the river, the hidden preserve lies below you.

Begin at Mink River Road in the heart of Ellison Bay across from the Pioneer Store. This turn-of-the-century convenience market was built in 1900 and still retains its authentic charm and character. You'll be following Mink River Road to its conclusion at Waters End Road. Turn right on Waters End Road, pass over ZZ, then turn right on Old Stage Road. Pass over County Z to Highview and turn right. Take Highview to Lakeview. Turn left on Lakeview back to Mink River Road and turn left for the trip back.

Newport Park Pedaling (11.5 miles)

Tour the "top of the thumb" along Garrett Bay and Hedgehog Harbor through winding wooded hills, meadows, forest and farmland. Stop at the Gills Rock ferry dock for a smoked fish lunch if you like, before heading back.

Beginning at the Newport State Park visitor contact station, head out of the park on South Newport Lane. Turn left on Newport Drive and continue straight past the sign marking the turn to Highway 42. You'll pass Juice Mill Lane as Newport Drive makes a sharp corner at the Schoenbrunn (Mink River) Nature Conservancy.

MINK RIVER
ROLLING
BICYCLE TOUR

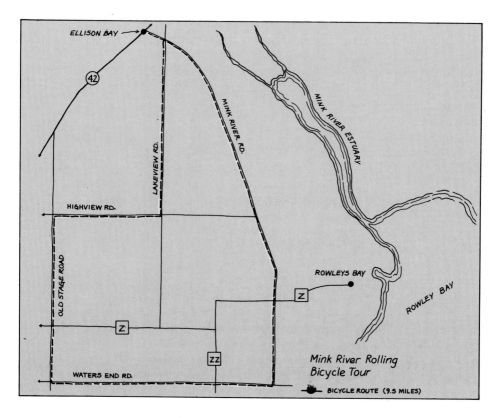

Mink River Rolling Bicycle Tour

BICYCLE ROUTE (9.5 MILES)

NEWPORT PARK
PEDALING
BICYCLING TOUR

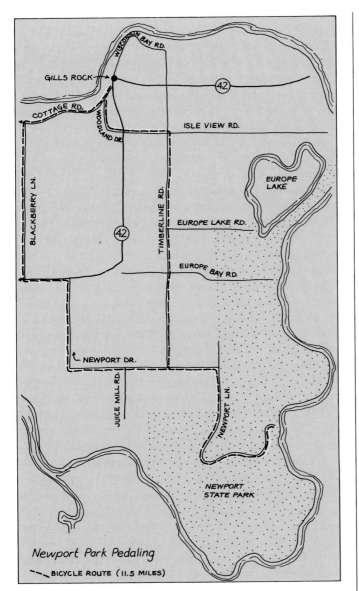

Newport Park Pedaling

BICYCLE ROUTE (11.5 MILES)

Continue to Highway 42, and turn left on this busy road for two blocks, then turn right on Blackberry Lane. Continue on Blackberry up the two short hills and cruise down this beautiful bluff to Cottage Road. When you reach Highway 42, a left turn will take you to the Gills Rock Ferry. A right turn up Highway 42 continues your journey. Near the crest of Highway 42 turn left on Isle View Road and head three blocks to Timberline. Turn right on Timberline, then left on Newport Drive. Turn left on Newport Lane and head back to your starting point.

CANOE AND KAYAK ROUTES

Europe Lake

Europe Lake is a rare treasure. Much of the lake's eastern shoreline is part of Newport State Park, the exception being a family-owned resort just east of the boat landing. Its wild shoreline, sand bottom and limited development make Europe Lake a very appealing family canoe trip. When the water is low an excellent warm-water beach greets paddlers, but be sure you're on park property if you leave your canoe. Newport State Park has two campsites on Europe Lake accessible by canoe, but you can't leave your car overnight at the boat launch. That means someone has to move the car to the park and hike in. To get to the put-in, take Highway 42 north of Ellison Bay to Europe Bay Road. Take Europe Bay Road to Timberline Road, go left on Timberline to Europe Lake Road, and turn right to the boat launch. It takes about a half day to paddle around the lake. Beginners and up can accomplish it, and summer is the best season.

KANGAROO LAKE
Kangaroo Lake takes its name from its unusual shape. This spring-fed lake is Door County's largest inland body of water. It contains walleye, bass, northern pike, perch and other panfish.

Kangaroo Lake

Kangaroo Lake is a shallow, spring-fed, warm-water jewel best seen by canoe at sunset. You can spend an hour or a full day here admiring the woods, the cottages and the waterfowl. The lake reaches a maximum depth of 13 feet and covers 1,100 acres. Northern pike, walleye, largemouth bass and panfish constitute the fishery. Waterfowl use 340 acres of adjoining wetland for resting and nesting. This wetland is also accessible by canoe with a carry over the causeway that supports County E.

Kangaroo Lake occupies the depression left by glacial

Lake Nippissing, and sand dunes now separate Kangaroo Lake and Lake Michigan. Heins Creek, a spring-fed stream in serious need of permanent protection, flows to Lake Michigan from a three-foot dam at the outlet from Kangaroo Lake. Much of the shoreline, including the island in the middle of Kangaroo Lake, is privately owned. Swimming, however, is popular at the boat landing, and a sand bottom cushions the feet of those venturing to take a dip. Beginners and up can enjoy this trip spring, summer or fall.

The put-in is the boat landing off O'Brien Road. Exit Highway 57 north of Jacksonport at Logerquist Road. Turn right (east) on O'Brien Road to the public boat landing. Or, a canoe launch is possible from the causeway on County E that divides Kangaroo Lake. Exit Highway 57 south of Baileys Harbor west on County E to the causeway.

Clark Lake

Whitefish Dunes State Park occupies a portion of the southeastern shore of Clark Lake and waterfowl appreciate the wooded wetland bordering this lake. With a maximum depth of 25 feet, Clark Lake is the deepest of the mainland lakes on the Door Peninsula (Mackaysee Lake on Chambers Island is a bit deeper) and it supports an excellent fishery that includes walleye, northern pike, yellow perch and panfish.

The wind likes to whip up small waves on this wide 864-acre lake, but even beginners should have little trouble getting to shore if the weather turns poor. Clark Lake, like other inland lakes on the peninsula, occupies a depression left by glacial Lake Nippissing. The water is clear and the dunes separating Clark Lake from Lake Michigan are part of Whitefish Dunes State Park, ensuring preservation of this geologic wonder. An inlet stream called Logan Creek, which also merits protection, enters Clark Lake from the Lost Lake wetland northwest of here. Draining the lake is Whitefish Bay Creek, a turquoise-colored stream that flows in beautiful contrast to the dark forest that lines

CLARK LAKE
Clark Lake is the deepest of the inland lakes on the Door County mainland. This 868-acre lake is home to walleye, northern pike, smallmouth bass, perch, bluegill, rockbass and carp.

The sandy area of Clark Lake is actually a bay-mouth bar separating this inland lake from Lake Michigan. As the waters of ancient glacial Lake Nippissing receded, a bar of sand built up across the front of a shallow bay and eventually isolated what is now Clark Lake.

its banks.

To get to the put-in, exit Highway 57 north of Sturgeon Bay at Clark Lake Road (en route to Whitefish Dunes State Park).

Mud Lake

Mud Lake is a joy to experience by canoe. Undeveloped marsh, abundant waterfowl and a pristine natural setting provide a scenic treat for those who make the effort to explore it.

The lake itself is just over one mile long and about a half mile wide (155 acres), but it is surrounded by 750 acres of cedar, conifer and aspen that form its wooded wetland border. Over 1,000 acres of this ecosystem have been designated the Mud Lake Scientific Area, ensuring its continued protection. The maximum depth here is five feet, but over half the lake is less than three feet deep. Marl, a form of soft, spongy soil, lines the lake floor, making a departure from your boat regrettable.

Birding is a popular activity here since bald eagles, ospreys, peregrine falcons, Cooper's hawks and red-shouldered hawks are likely to use this area for feeding and resting during migration.

This is a popular waterfowl hunting spot in the fall, and canoeists are likely to find duck blinds as they venture the one mile up Reibolt's Creek to Mud Lake.

Current and wind can sometimes make travel a little rough on Reibolt's Creek, but when the rain is falling and the ducks are flying low, you may have hit just the perfect time for a Mud Lake getaway.

To get there, exit Highway 57 on County Q at Baileys Harbor. Launch where Reibolt's Creek enters Moonlight Bay and paddle upstream to Mud Lake. Public parking is available.

Cave Point Cruise

For sea kayakers, Whitefish Dunes provides the best surfing beach on the peninsula. When whitecaps are breaking, wet or dry suits are recommended. Under calm seas, beginners will find the sand bottom and clear water inviting and nonthreatening. From the boat landing at the end of County T, paddlers heading north (left) will pass a series of summer homes before reaching Whitefish Dunes State Park. The tallest of these mountains of sand reaches 93 feet, and parking your boat on the beach for a hike is a great way to take a break.

Kayakers continuing on should be confident of their skills. Once Cave Point is rounded, waves deflecting from the cliffs become confused and unpredictable during even moderate weather conditions. However, this is an exceptionally beautiful area where Lake Michigan waves have eroded the limestone cliffs to form cave-like configurations. Rescue here is diffficult and a capsize could be disastrous. If a shuttle vehicle is available, Schauer Town Park, off Cave Point Road north of Cave Point County Park, provides a convenient take-out point.

To get to the put-in on Whitefish Bay, exit Highway 57 north of Sturgeon Bay on County T in Valmy. Head east on County T until you see Lake Michigan and the boat landing. Navigation chart: NOAA #14910.

Mink River

This route, best undertaken by intermediates in a canoe or kayak, explores the beautiful Mink River Estuary. The Nature Conservancy says this is the last remaining high-quality estuary on Lake Michigan.

Preserved for future generations, this 1,500-acre eco-system is unique. Bulrushes protect the wetlands from the waves and tidal effect of Lake Michigan. The wetlands contain plants threatened with extinction in Wisconsin. As many as 200 species of birds may use this area during migration. The waters provide a spawning ground for several kinds of fish, and fishing in season is excellent for both bass and Lake Michigan species.

To get there you can take County Z to the Wagon Trail Resort and use its landing on Rowley's Bay (fee charged). Alternately, you can put in at Sand Bay Park Beach located off Water's End Road east of Sister Bay.

WHITEFISH BAY CREEK
Whitefish Bay Creek is a one-mile-long outlet stream that drains Clark Lake, flowing through a cedar swamp into Lake Michigan. During high water, rainbow, brown and brook trout enter the creek.

Many paddlers prefer this put-in since the park provides convenient parking and no launch fee is charged. Either put-in requires paddlers to follow the shoreline north. Wind is a problem for canoes here, as are waves once you leave the bay just before heading into the Mink River, but sea kayakers should have little trouble. A third alternative put-in requires a very long portage (scout first), but avoids the open water of Lake Michigan. To reach this turn right on Newport Drive off Highway 42 north of Ellison Bay. Look for the sign at the corner where Newport Drive turns sharply left. That's the one-half-mile-long Hemlock Trail to "Indian Joe" landing on the Mink River. Navigation chart: NOAA #14909.

Europe Bay

A convenient put-in and a long pristine sand beach add up to a delightful day trip for beginning kayakers on this shoreline paddle. Europe Bay Beach is part of Newport State Park. Quiet observers may encounter wildlife along the shore since many animals make their homes in the rocky ledges as the beach gives way to rocky steps and cedar forest. Rounding the point, kayakers will find a day-use picnic area in this park. Backcountry campsites are available, but check with the ranger before setting up camp at Newport State Park. If it's June, July or August, make reservations in advance to ensure a site.

To get to the put-in at Europe Bay Town Park, exit Highway 42 east of Ellison Bay at Europe Bay Road. (Follow the signs for Newport State Park.) Follow Europe Bay Road to its conclusion at the beach. Navigation chart: NOAA #14909.

Dunes Lake

Dunes Lake is one of the hidden treasures of Door County. Remote and captivating, this 81-acre wetland lake is the centerpiece of what the Nature Conservancy says could be the largest, contiguous cedar swamp in Wisconsin. The only access to this shallow lake is by canoe or kayak via a delightful one-mile paddle down twisting Donlan's Creek. After putting in at the Haberli Road bridge you'll leave the developed world behind for a winding dip past painted turtles and marsh marigolds before the creek succumbs to spendid Dunes Lake. Fringed with cattails, rushes and sedges, Dune's Lake demands a low impact visit. Paddlers are prohibited from stepping out of their boats for any reason since the entire shore of Donlan's Creek and Dune's Lake remain in private ownership.

Shivering Sands Creek drains the lake affording additional paddling opportunities for those anxious to explore farther. Over 110 bird species frequent this complex including sandhill cranes, black terns and osprey. The ecological importance of this site has attracted the interest of the Nature Conservancy which is working with local landowners to protect the entire 3,400 acre complex.

To reach the put-in, exist Highway 57 at Institute on Country View Lane. Turn on Haberli Road and look for the bridge crossing Donlan's Creek. There is limited parking. Paddle south to Dunes Lake.

DOOR COUNTY SOILS

The soils and geology of the Door Peninsula present unique problems. Since the mantle of soil is so thin in most areas and the bedrock is in fractured layers, bacterial contamination of well water can occur. One family septic tank here can contaminate the drinking water of many wells.

CITIES, TOWNS AND VILLAGES

Baileys Harbor (pop. 827)

The village takes its name from its founder, Captain Justin Bailey, a schooner pilot who discovered the harbor's safe haven during a fierce Lake Michigan gale in 1848. After waiting out the squall, Bailey explored the mainland, loading timber and building stone aboard his ship before continuing his journey south. Bailey's glowing report of this natural harbor prompted his employer, Alanson Sweet, to build a pier and open a stone quarry here in 1849, shipping timber and building stone south to Milwaukee. Mr. Sweet turned out to be quite a promoter, persuading the Wisconsin State Legislature to define the boundaries of Door County and designate Baileys Harbor the county seat. Sweet attempted to change the name of the village to Gibraltar, but the change never took hold, and when Sturgeon Bay assumed the title of Door County seat in 1857, Captain Bailey regained his namesake.

Visitors to modern Baileys Harbor will find rugged shore, soggy swamp and virgin forest protected as a national landmark within the boundaries of Ridges Sanctuary, Toft Point Nature Conservancy, and the Mud Lake Wildlife Area. It is here that the wild, untamed land that Captain Bailey found so inviting retains its natural appeal. Just southwest of Baileys Harbor, visitors can explore Kangaroo Lake, the largest inland lake on the peninsula. Located just southwest of Baileys Harbor, Kangaroo is an inviting, shallow, spring-fed lake. The 1,100-acre lake occupies a shallow depression left by glacial Lake Nippissing eons ago. Even though much of the shoreline of Kangaroo Lake, including an island rising from its center, is privately owned, swimming, canoeing and fishing remain popular pastimes.

Northern pike, walleye, largemouth bass and panfish occupy the lake providing a challenge to the fishermen who launch their canoes from the public boat landing or dangle a worm from shore. The public boat landing, located off O'Brien Road, also provides swimmers access to the lake. The water of this inland lake warms earlier in the year than Lake Michigan and its sand bottom provides comfort to the feet.

Cradled between North Bay and Moonlight Bay, the recently approved Baileys Harbor Boreal Forest State Natural Area and Moonlight Bay Bedrock Beach Natural Area preserve rare plants and wild lakeshore.

Nearby, visitors can explore Cana Island Lighthouse. Rich in history and scenic in character, Cana Island is a wonderful place to ponder the past and plot the future where the woods and water whisper on the quiet side of Door County.

A breakwater adds to the natural protection of Baileys Harbor.

For information, visit the Baileys Harbor Visitor Information Center located in the Town Hall in the center of Baileys Harbor or write: Baileys Harbor Information Center, P.O. Box 31, Baileys Harbor, WI 54202; or phone: 920-839-2366. The library/town hall phone: 920-839-2210.

Boynton "Bjorklunden" Estate

Visitors are welcome to tour the Bjorklunden Chapel from 1–4 on Mondays and Wednesdays from mid-June through August. A nominal admission is charged. Other times are available upon special request. For more information contact the Bjorklunden resident director at 920-839-2216.

To reach Bjorklunden, follow Highway 57 through Jacksonport. Just south of Baileys Harbor follow the marked private gravel road to the "birch forest by the lakeshore."

Baileys Harbor Ridges Town Park: Immediately north of the village off Ridges Drive on Lake Michigan, this 30-acre park is adjacent to Ridges Sanctuary. There are picnic places and a great sand beach.

Anclam Town Park: This small park is located between Highway 57 and Lake Michigan in the village. There are picnic facilities with playground equipment, a small sand beach, restrooms and a boat ramp. Fishing is popular from the point for trout and salmon.

Baileys Harbor Fire Station Field: Adjacent to the village fire station, this 1.5-acre park offers tennis courts.

Baileys Harbor Recreation Field: Located off Summit Road west of the village with a baseball field and picnic facilities.

Village of Jacksonport (pop. 744)

The Village of Jacksonport lies halfway between the North Pole and the Equator, making it a pleasant

STONE FENCES
Stone fences became boundaries as land was cleared, and serve the same purpose today. Composed of glacial rock, these fences tell a tale of hard labor and long days on peninsula farms.

crossroads for people to plan their future paths. Just south of the village lies Cave Point County Park. When Lake Michigan is venting its wrath here, you'll find geyser-like sprays erupting from the limestone ledges in a tribute to nature's forces.

Surrounding Cave Point is Whitefish Dunes State Park, another "must see" locale, and home to the largest sand dunes on the western shore of Lake Michigan. You'll need a state park vehicle sticker to park here, but it's worth the price of admission when the sun is blazing and the waves are rolling in.

Jacksonport today is a close-knit community of farmers and merchants proud of their German lineage. They commemorate this heritage each August when antique farming equipment is exhibited at a local farm during the Thresheree. Another popular event is the annual Maifest Celebration over Memorial Day weekend when a cold brew and a hot bratwurst will have you dancing a polka.

Jacksonport Town Park: On County V east of the village, this park sports a baseball diamond.

Lyle Harter-Matter Sanctuary: The sanctuary is a 40-acre undeveloped wildlife area, completely wooded. It's located off Highway 57 north of Jacksonport.

Meridian County Park: Just north of Jacksonport, contiguous with Lyle Harter-Matter Sanctuary, this park is located halfway between the North Pole and the Equator. The park is heavily wooded with a wayside picnic area.

Lakeside Town Park: Located on the lakeshore off Highway 57 in the village, this park is the site of various summer festivities and has a nice sand beach.

Schauer Town Park: On Lake Michigan south of Jacksonport via Cave Point Road and Schauer Road, this small park (1.5 acres) provides a boat ramp.

ISLANDS

JACKSON HARBOR RIDGES

ROCK ISLAND
STATE PARK

SCHOOLHOUSE BEACH TOWN PARK

ROCK ISLAND BEACH

MOUNTAIN ROAD TOWN PARK

JACKSON HARBOR DUNES
TOWN PARK & BEACH

EASTSIDE CTY. PARK & BEACH

WASHINGTON ISLAND
ATHLETIC FIELD

SAND DUNES TOWN PARK & BEACH

DOOR BLUFF HEADLAND
COUNTY PARK

WISCONSIN BAY
TOWN PARK

PORTES DES MORTS TOWN PARK

42

STATE PARKS
TOWN, VILLAGE & COUNTY PARKS
PRESERVES
BEACHES

Z

ZZ

ZZ

Through the Windshield

AN OVERVIEW OF THE ISLANDS

WASHINGTON
ISLAND CHAMBER
OF COMMERCE
RR 1, Box 222,
Washington Island, WI
54246. Phone:
920-847-2146.

The islands that dot the sparkling waters surrounding the tip of the Door Peninsula invite exploration. Called collectively the Grand Traverse Chain, these islands separate Wisconsin's Door Peninsula from Michigan's Garden Peninsula. Historically, Plum, Washington and Rock islands served as points of refuge for fur traders and voyageurs paddling the route between the Straits of Mackinac and the Mississippi River.

The Grand Traverse islands are glacially worn remnants of the ancient drainage separating the Green Bay and Lake Michigan basins. When bedrock is not directly exposed, it is covered by a thin layer of sand and silt that anchors the trees that shelter birds and wildlife. Of the eight islands and eight islets comprising the Grand Traverse Chain, about half are in Wisconsin and half are in Michigan.

A proposal to incorporate the five Wisconsin islands separating Green Bay from Lake Michigan into a state park or National Lakeshore has been discussed in the past but, unfortunately, the plan has no current initiative. The logical headquarters for such a park would be Washington Island. Beaches, bluffs, ridges and woodlands bring thousands of visitors to this 36-square-mile island each year. Most of the 75 miles of road are paved, and bringing a car or bicycle to the island allows you the freedom to explore at your leisure. Excursions to Washington Island begin at the tip of the Door Peninsula mainland with departures from either Gills Rock or the Northport Pier.

Sandwiched by Death's Door Bluff to the west and Table Bluff to the east, the harbor at Gills Rock provides a striking panorama. Early risers will find charter captains and commercial fishermen chugging out of the harbor in search of whitefish, trout and salmon. The car ferries that transport autos to Washington Island no longer dock here, but those wishing to tour the island by bicycle or guided tour can meet the 65-foot *Yankee Clipper* here from late May

(overleaf)

A sailboat awaits her captain at Fish Creek.

through mid-October (phone: 920-854-2972) or the *C. G. Richter* run by a competing ferry service (phone: 920-847-2546 or 800-223-2094.) Competing tour "trains" also meet both the *Yankee Clipper* and the *C. G. Richter*, providing a narrated 90-minute tour of the island. Those wishing to conduct their own tours are welcome to bring their bicycles aboard, although bike or moped rentals are available on the island. A third ship departing Gills Rock brings visitors to historic Fayette State Park on Michigan's Garden Peninsula. The *Island Clipper* sails Thursdays from mid-July through mid-August, taking visitors past the entire Grand Traverse Island Chain, including Washington, Rock, St. Martin, Poverty, and Big and Little Summer islands. Reservations are recommended (phone: 920-854-2972). The *Island Clipper* can accommodate a limited number of sea kayaks aboard and paddlers have been known to board the vessel with their boats for a one way trip to Fayette paddling back to Gills Rock over the course of several days. Once visitors complete the one hour, 45-minute crossing to Fayette, they dock for three hours at Snail Shell Harbor, where there are opportunities to tour the historic park, swim or enjoy a picnic lunch prior to the cruise back.

Continuing on Highway 42 you'll wind your way to the Northport Pier. You can credit landscape architect Jens Jenson for this scenic and unique drive. Instead of mowing down the forest to provide a perfect blacktop straightaway, Jenson convinced Door County officials to curve this wooded drive into a series of winding bends that seem to flow through the woods, becoming part of the landscape rather than altering it. Just prior to the ferry dock a town road leads to Porte des Morts Park. This town park preserves Table Bluff and also traces its conception to Jens Jenson. Jenson, a member of the Door County Parks Committee, envisioned preserving all of the county's bluffs as parkland. As you stand overlooking Washington and Plum islands, the reason for his crusade becomes apparent.

Entering Northport you'll see a line forming to board the Washington Island car ferry on the far right of the roadway. These car ferries, which include the Robert

THE DEATH'S DOOR LEGEND

The six-mile passage separating Washington Island from the mainland takes its forboding name from Native American war parties who called this passage "Door to Death" because of the havoc the currents and weather could wreak upon their fragile canoes. French explorers shared the Indians' respect for this strait, translating the native term into Porte des Morts, or "Death's Door." Today, Coast Guard navigation aids guide both commercial and private vessels through the passage in safety and comfort.

Nobel, Eyrarbakki and Washington, serve as the island's lifeline, shuttling food, mail, equipment, visitors and residents across the Porte des Morts strait. During July and August the Washington Island Ferry Line offers more than 20 round trips daily, tapering off to five trips in September and only one round trip daily during January, February and March. Reservations are recommended during the winter months but unnecessary during summer (phone: 920-847-2546). You're welcome to bring your bike or kayak on board for an extra $1.50. Bringing your car across will set you back about $17 round trip plus the passenger fare of about $8.00 each. Those wishing to save the expense of personal transportation can take advantage of the Cherry Train Tour. A combination ferry and Cherry Train Tour runs about $13 and includes a 90-minute narrated tour of the island in an open-air "train."

DETROIT ISLAND
Peace-loving Potawatomi Indians would frequently hide on Detroit Island when bands of marauding tribes invaded their Rock Island territory.

Boating across Death's Door Passage you'll see tiny Pilot Island to the east. For more than 40 years Pilot Island lived up to its name, providing a lighthouse that served as the only guide through these treacherous waters until a similar beacon was erected on Plum Island in 1886. Pilot Island, although federally owned, is privately leased. The 600-acre island immediately ahead is Plum Island, so named because it lies "plumb" in the middle of Death's Door Strait. For over one hundred years the Coast Guard operated a manned station here deriving its electrical power by underground cable from the mainland. In the mid-1990s the Coast Guard moved its operations to Washington Island, leaving this beautiful island to the resident white-tailed deer and waterfowl which make their homes here. In past years the unchecked population of the white-tails and their voracious appetites has threatened island vegetation. There is an outstanding shallow harbor frequented by waterfowl on the northwest corner of the island. Private vessels were once welcome to dock here and visit the grounds, but since the departure of the Coast Guard visitation is off limits.

Chugging closer to Washington Island, Detroit Island looms ahead, guarding the entrance to Detroit Harbor

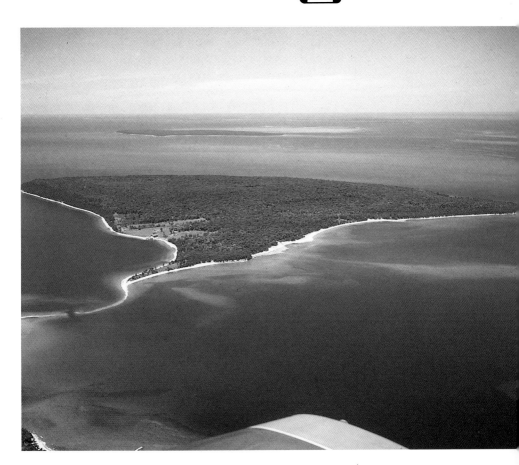

and sheltering the ferry dock from vicious storms and swells. Detroit Island is privately owned and the independent folks that summer here depend on their own transportation to reach their homesteads. The island is not served by the Washington Island Electric Co-op; residents depend on diesel fuel to generate electrical power.

Wheeling off the Washington Island Ferry you'll arrive on Pt. Lobdell Road. Bicycle rentals, tour train connections, shops and restaurants are located within walking distance of the landing. If you have a private vehicle or bicycle, this is where your island tour begins. Heading straight (north) on Pt. Lobdell Road you'll pass through a lovely forested grove with wide shoulders to accommodate bicyclists. Proceed 1.8 miles to Main

Rock Island is part of the Grand Traverse Island Chain. This archipelago stretches from Wisconsin's Door to Michigan's Delta peninsulas. St. Martin Island is visible in the distance.

Road and turn left. Main Road comes as close to a "downtown" as Washington Island has to offer. Development and attractions on the island are spread out, but clustered along Main Road is the post office, grocery store and island schools. Adjacent to the Washington Island School you'll find one of the best equipped indoor public recreation centers on the Door Peninsula. Opened in 1988, the Washington Island Recreation Center boasts a four-lane swimming pool, whirlpool, locker room and exercise facility stocked with state-of-the-art equipment. This wonderful facility is the result of a one-million-dollar donation by John and Jane Mosling. The Moslings donated additional funds to maintain the facility and the result is striking. Visitors are charged a small fee for use of the center. Both daily and seasonal vacation passes are available. Hours vary depending on the season (phone: 920-847-2226).

If you wish to camp on Washington Island, you'll be sidetracking by turning right on Lake View Road just past the recreation center. Island Camping and Recreation is a 100-site private campground leased to the Town of Washington Island. Long-range plans call for the Town to purchase this campground which is the only facility where you can pitch a tent or wheel in an RV on Washington Island. To make reservations or find out the latest status, call the Town of Washington office at 920-847-2522.

Continuing your tour, following Main Road you'll pass the Deer Run Golf resort. This par-35, nine-hole course is open to the public, offering clubs and carts for rent (phone: 920-847-2017). At the intersection of Jackson Harbor Road you'll find the Washington Island Art and Nature Center. Open daily from mid-June through August, including autumn Sundays, the Art and Nature Center offers exhibits and a short nature trail identifying island plants and environments. The center is a nonprofit, educational organization supported by donations, grants and memberships. A small admission fee is charged. Proceeding on Main Road you'll reach the intersection of Little Lake Road, which leads to Little Lake, and the Jacobsen Museum. Donated to

FISHING MUSEUM
Located as Jackson Harbor, the Town Fishing Museum displays fishing artifacts and commercial processing equipment in a museum setting.

Washington Island in memory of Jens Jacobsen, these scenic grounds and interesting museum recall island history in a cedar log building. The museum is open weekends from Memorial Day through mid-June; from mid-June daily through August; and weekends again through fall. A curator is on hand to answer your questions and offer advice. A small admission fee is charged. There is also carry-in boat access to Little Lake adjacent to the museum. Those without a canoe can walk out on the dock for a pleasant view of this ancient glacial lake.

Backtracking on Little Lake Road you'll reach Jackson Harbor Road where you'll turn left (east). After a short jaunt down Jackson Harbor Road you'll reach a turnoff to Schoolhouse Beach. This town park offers a pebble beach and picnicking facilities in a beautiful setting overlooking Washington Harbor. The beach here is not well suited to young children since the drop-off is quite steep. Advanced swimmers, however, will enjoy taking advantage of the swim raft anchored offshore during the summer season.

Heading back down Jackson Harbor Road you'll discover the Washington Island Farm Museum. This free museum recalls the history of farming on the island. There is an original log building on the grounds stocked with hand tools used by the pioneers who carved out a living on this rugged island. The Farm Museum is open daily from Memorial Day weekend through October. Continuing on Jackson Harbor Road you'll pass Range Line Road before turning right on Mountain Road. Mountain Road leads to Mountain Park Lookout. A sturdy wooden staircase, donated by an islander and completed in 1989, climbs a steep hillside to an observation tower on top of the "mountain." The staircase eliminates the need to climb the steep trail that folks had to previously endure just to reach the observation tower, where another climb awaits. Your efforts will be rewarded when you reach the summit of the observation deck, which provides a stunning view of the island, Lake Michigan and points beyond.

Backtracking on Mountain Road and turning right on Jackson Harbor Road you'll pass Sievers Looms and

WASHINGTON ISLAND FACTS

Washington Island has about 550 year-round residents and about 3,000 summer residents. Nearly 78% of the island is owned by non-residents. About 15 new homes are built each year.

School. This unique island business produces spinning and weaving looms in its woodworking shop. The Sievers School of Fiber Arts has more than 30 instructors who conduct both weekday and weekend classes during the summer and fall. Housing facilities are available for registered students (phone: 920-847-2264). Behind Sievers lies the rich and remote Coffey Swamp. This beautiful private wetland is inaccessible to the public but certainly merits permanent protection. Proceeding, Jackson Harbor Road leads to picturesque Jackson Harbor. The commercial fishing docks, boats and hard-working fishermen add to the distinct flavor of Jackson Harbor. This is where you can board the Karfi for the ten-minute trip to Rock Island State Park. No cars are allowed on this historic 900-acre preserve, but it's a wonderful place to spend an hour, a day or a week hiking, swimming, picnicking or camping. Just south of the state ferry dock you'll find Jackson Harbor Ridges. The Ridges, a state of Wisconsin Scientific Area, offers an outstanding example of beach, dune, boreal and shore meadow communities. A hiking trail crosses this town property and provides ample opportunity for careful exploration.

For the trip back to the car ferry dock, backtrack on Jackson Harbor Road to Deer Lane Road. This paved, wooded road is appropriately named since the white-tail population on the island is substantial and opportunities to spot deer, especially at sunset, are plentiful. From Deer Lane Road you'll be turning right on Town Line Road for a jaunt through the heart of Washington Island. At Range Line Road, turn left and you'll be heading back to Detroit Harbor Road where a right turn leads back to the ferry dock. If you're up for a swim, continue on Range Line Road past the marina to South Shore Drive. Just before the pavement turns to gravel you'll encounter Sand Dunes Town Park. The superb public beach here offers the best swimming opportunities on the island. Even if you're not up for a dip this park merits a visit, if only to sink your feet in sand and recall your island memories.

ISLAND LODGING
Washington Island offers year-round overnight accommodations including hotels, motels, cottages and a campground. For detailed information write: Washington Island Chamber of Commerce, Box 80, Washington Island, WI 54246. Phone: 920-847-2225.

STATE PARKS

Rock Island State Park

This Lake Michigan island park is located off the north-east shore of Washington Island and is accessible by boat only. Commercial ferry service is available from Washington Island and private boat docking is allowed. Washington Island Ferry phone: 920-847-2546. Karfi (Rock Island) Ferry phone: 920-847-2425 or 920-847-2252. The address: Rock Island State Park, Washington Island, WI 54246. Phone: 920-847-2235.

FACILITIES:
There are 35 primitive campsites and five hike-in campsites. All campsites are reservable.

RECREATION:
There are hiking trails, nature trails, an excellent sand beach, a historic lighthouse and a cemetery to investigate. The island is equipped with pit toilets, drinking water and picnic facilities. The park is open late spring through early fall.

Rock Island is a world class hideaway, cushioned by the reefs, waves and wind of Lake Michigan. The park's isolation, unique geography and fascinating plant life make this peaceful preserve a place to cherish.

The 900-acre island is one link in the 16-island Grand Traverse chain which spans the 27-mile watery wilderness separating Wisconsin's Door Peninsula from Michigan's Garden Peninsula. It was this magnificent isolation which protected Potawatomi Indians from marauding invaders and provided a natural canoeing route or "Grand Traverse" for French explorers and fur traders. It was also this splendid seclusion that attracted Rock Island's most famous twentieth century resident conservationist Chester Thordarson.

In 1910 Thordarson purchased the entire island with the exception of the 129 acres the federal government owned surrounding Potawatomi Lighthouse on the island's northern shore. Over the next twenty years he cleared and landscaped a small section of the island

CAMPING
State parks in Door County offer over 600 campsites, ranging from full-service units to backpacking sites. During the summer, reservations are recommended. Private campgrounds offer an additional 1,000-plus sites, so you'll always find a place to stake out your claim to Door County.

while overseeing the Icelandic-style construction of a massive stone "Great Hall" above a boat house at the island's landing dock. In 1964 the State of Wisconsin purchased the island from Thordarson's heirs to forever preserve this natural kingdom as Rock Island State Park.

Today, Thordarson's awesome limestone "Great Hall" still stands serving as the park's nature center. It once housed Thordarson's personal library, including a valuable compilation of rare books which now rest in the University of Wisconsin collection.

Perhaps of even greater importance to what Thordarson built is what the inventive genius chose not to develop. He left all but 30 acres of the island in its natural state, and a hike down the island's trails will quickly reveal the inventor's second passion: botany.

Rock Island is a living classroom. A stroll through the forest revives the senses and frees the mind to wander. Beneath the forest canopy of sugar maple, white birch, basswood and white cedar you'll discover a hidden retreat for wildlife and traveler alike. Wild strawberries flourish in season and quiet hikers will frequently startle resident white-tailed deer grazing at sunset.

Rock Island is a land of striking geographic diversity. On the western side of the island huge cliffs plunge into Lake Michigan while on its eastern shore you'll find a one-half-mile-long sand beach flanked by sand dunes. On the island's northern edge the Niagara escarpment stretches over 200 feet above Lake Michigan before surrendering to Lake Michigan's pebble shore at its base. It is here you'll find the recently restored Potawatomi Lighthouse looming high over the blue water expanse which separates Wisconsin's Rock from Michigan's St. Martin Island. Built in 1836, this was the first lighthouse in Wisconsin; and of even greater significance, the first on Lake Michigan. David Corbin served as the original keeper of the light, tending the beacon for sixteen lonely years. Corbin died in 1852 and his remains are buried, perhaps fittingly, in an unmarked grave on the lighthouse grounds.

Rock Island has not always been kind to intruders.

ROCK ISLAND
STATE PARK

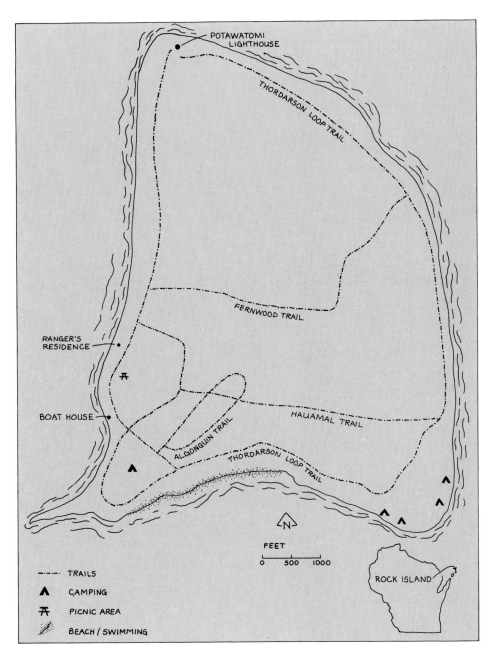

POTAWATOMI
LIGHTHOUSE

THORDARSON LOOP TRAIL

FERNWOOD TRAIL

RANGER'S
RESIDENCE

HAUAMAL TRAIL

BOAT HOUSE

ALGONQUIN TRAIL

THORDARSON LOOP TRAIL

N

FEET
0   500   1000

- — - — TRAILS

⋀   CAMPING

⊼   PICNIC AREA

░   BEACH / SWIMMING

ROCK ISLAND

A pioneer cemetery can be found along the park's southeastern shore and the headstone dates reveal a land of harsh winters, short summers and scarce medical attention.

Most visitors arrive via commercial ferry from Washington Island, although docking your private vessel or arriving by sea kayak at Rock Island is permitted. If you're a camper, the most convenient (and expensive) method of getting to Rock Island requires that you take your car aboard the Washington Island Ferry from Northport Pier. Once on Washington Island you must drive (see Washington Island map) to Jackson Harbor where you will board the Karfi for the ten-minute trip to Rock Island. Alternatives include paddling to Rock Island through Death's Door Passage, a difficult, challenging trip; pedaling from Detroit Harbor to Jackson Harbor—tough, but possible with the right camping gear; or snagging a taxi on Washington Island for the trip to Jackson Harbor. Regarding this last alternative, check with Vi's Taxi on Washington Island (920-847-2283). Vi has been known to shuttle campers, but call first.

Biking the trails on Rock Island is not permitted but you are welcome to bring you bike to the island for safe keeping. Keep this in mind if you choose to pedal to Jackson Harbor from where the Washington Island Ferry docks.

Backpackers receive special attention on Rock Island with five campsites set aside to provide them with the peace and quiet they relish. Hikers will find room to roam with well-developed trails of various lengths that provide an interesting variety of flora and fauna. Day hikes are the most popular method of viewing the island, and a three-day weekend should allow you to hike most of the trails and still spend an afternoon on the beach. Budget extra time for crossing to the mainland, and bring adequate gear to weather a rainstorm since you'll be on your own once you start enjoying "the island life."

GLACIAL GLOSSARY

Moraine: deposits of soil and rock material carried by a glacier and deposited at its edges when the glacier melted.

Kettle: a depression formed by a block of glacial ice that was buried in debris and later melted.

Drumlin: stream-lined, elongated hills composed of glacial till and paralleling the direction of flow of a glacier.

Esker: a long, sinuous ridge of stratified sand and gravel deposited by a stream that flowed through a tunnel at the base of a glacier.

(opposite page)
Sheer limestone cliffs rise 200 feet above Lake Michigan on the northern shore of Rock Island.

HIKING TRAILS

Thordarson Loop Trail: The Thordarson Loop (6.5 miles) is a great trail that takes hikers along a sand beach, over towering bluffs and along a rocky shore, presenting a sample of everything the island has to offer. This all-day hike is not to be rushed. You'll wish to pause for a picnic at the Potawatomi Lighthouse and take the steps down to the rocky shore. This trail can be hiked in either direction, but you may want to pack your swimsuit if you plan to return to the beach for a swim. Where the rocky ledges meet the sandy beach, be on the lookout for carvings on the small cliffs. They're hard to spot, but look closely and you'll find them.

Fernwood Trail: The 1.5-mile Fernwood Trail cuts the Thordarson Loop in half and provides a shortcut to the Potawatomi Lighthouse. An interesting stretch in its own right, the Fernwood Trail is aptly named. Quiet hikers on this trail may encounter white-tailed deer near dusk and dawn, but since they live on an island they know the escape routes well.

Hauamal Trail: The Hauamal Trail (1.5 miles) begins at the picnic area and crosses the Algonquin Nature Trail, providing access to the farthest backpacking site on the island. This trail can also be combined with the Thordarson Trail to make a pleasant and interesting loop.

Algonquin Nature Trail: Even visitors spending just an hour on Rock Island will have time to hike the one-mile Algonquin Nature Trail. This self-guided, one-way hike will both educate and entertain.

Grand Traverse Islands Park

A proposal to incorporate the chain of islands off the tip of Door County into parkland remains a grand idea stalled in the water by government bureaucracy and priority changes. The islands—Plum, Pilot, Detroit,

Washington, Hog and Rock—form the southern link in the Grand Traverse Islands Chain. Off Michigan's Garden Peninsula, the islands Little Summer, Summer, Poverty and St. Martin form the northern link. These islands are rich in history and stirring in beauty. This outstanding string of island pearls remains largely undeveloped, but without permanent protection this historic link between Wisconsin and Michigan remains in peril.

To date, only Rock and Washington Island accommodate overnight visitors. Plum Island, so named because it lies "plumb" in the middle of Death's Door Passage, was once home to a manned Coast Guard station but this operation was moved to Washington Island in the mid-1990s. In 1987, Wisconsin had an opportunity to lease the island from the Coast Guard. One of the provisions of that lease called for the state to construct a chain link fence around the Coast Guard facilities. Because the state failed to appropriate the $30,000 necessary to build the fence the Coast Guard withdrew its offer, further delaying plans for Grand Traverse Island State Park. Today, Plum Island remains open to day trippers wishing to moor their boats at the Coast Guard dock or slide their kayaks up the beach.

For 45 years the lighthouse on nearby Pilot Island was the only beacon mariners could rely on to negotiate safe passage through the Portes des Morts Strait. In 1886, a similar lighthouse was erected on Plum Island. Detroit Island, another link in the Grand Traverse Chain, is a large, privately owned island with an interesting history. The first cabin built by white settlers in Door County stood (in 1834) near the northwest shore of this island. The Ottawa Indians who had lived there objected to the cabin since they had gardens and an ancestral burial grounds nearby. During a battle with these Indians one of the two builders of the cabin was killed and the other was rescued by a passing ship. The previous year, northern Michigan's famed "snowshoe priest," Bishop Frederic Baraga, visited the Ottawas and, at his urging, they built a bark chapel that he consecrated for their use.

BOBSLED RUN
During the late 1930s and early 1940s Peninsula State Park was home to ski jumps, ice rinks and even a bobsled run. The ski jump and a toboggan run were located on the park's north-facing escarpment, with the landing area near the present-day Nature Center.

Until about eighty years ago, Detroit Island was a storehouse of Indian relics. Burial mounds, well defined village sites, gardens, cairns and storage pits were found almost intact. All of this has been destroyed by souvenir hunters. Graves have been opened and plundered. Relics have been removed and burial grounds have been desecrated. Today, a handful of homesites stand along the shore but much of the island remains undeveloped.

Washington Island would serve as the logical headquarters for Grand Traverse Islands State Park. This island takes its name from a ship dispatched from Mackinac, Michigan, to establish a fort in Green Bay. The *Washington* was one of four schooners shuttling troops to the Door Peninsula in 1816. Arriving ahead of the other ships, the men of the *Washington* lay anchor off the island and named the harbor in which they were moored after their vessel. Although partially developed, Washington Island retains its enduring appeal. Boyer's Bluff, a spectacular wooded escarpment overlooking Lake Michigan, would make a fine addition to this proposed state park. The car ferries serving the island would provide a convenient link for further exploration of the Grand Traverse Chain.

The historic Potawatomi Lighthouse is found on the next link in the chain, Rock Island. Built in 1836, this lighthouse was the first navigational beacon operating in Wisconsin. During the 1850s and 1860s there was a school, church and even a doctor serving the island, which may have been the most populous settlement between Mackinac and Green Bay.

In 1910, Chicago industrialist Chester Thordarson, an Iceland native, purchased 661 acres on Rock Island for $5,735. In the late 1920s he built a magnificent boathouse and great hall that remain intact today. Thordarson proved to be an excellent steward of Rock Island and in 1964 the state of Wisconsin purchased his fine estate and the beautiful grounds surrounding it, establishing Rock Island State Park.

Crossing into Michigan you'll encounter St. Martin, Poverty, Summer and Little Summer islands completing the Grand Traverse Island Chain. These islands are

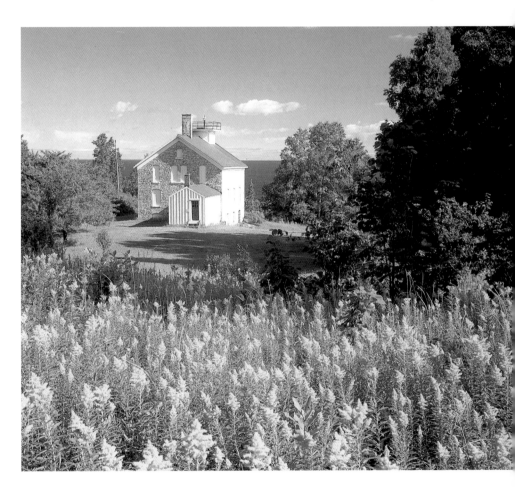

privately owned, and rumblings of development and even a condominium project continue to surface.

The idea behind a Grand Traverse Islands State or National Park has been bandied about for over a decade. Now only strong public support and courageous government leaders can turn this unique concept into a public treasure.

Perched above Rock Island, Potawatomi Lighthouse once served as the lonely outpost of a resident lighthouse keeper. Erected in 1836, this beacon is the oldest lighthouse in Wisconsin.

TOWN, VILLAGE AND COUNTY PARKS

Door Bluff Headlands County Park (155 acres)

This is the largest county park on the Door Peninsula (155 acres), and one of the least visited. The headlands are actually bluffs that rise from the waters of Green Bay. It features interesting flora, rugged unmarked trails and steep topography, making it a challenge to explore. The park is reached off Highway 42 via Cottage Road to Garrett Bay Road to Door Bluff Road.

Wisconsin Bay Town Park (5 acres)

This poorly marked town park offers a good view toward Washington Island. There is no beach and parking along the road is limited to only two cars.

Washington Island Athletic Field (4.4 acres)

Islanders take their summer baseball league very seriously, supporting them with zeal and enthusiasm. Chances are you'll get caught up in the action as well if you take in a game at the athletic field. Bleachers are provided and every seat in the house is a good one!

Sand Dunes Town Park (4 acres)

Access to the park is off South Shore Road about four miles east of the ferry dock. It has a great beach, and no crowds. Take the trail from the parking area up the hillside to the sand dunes and enjoy yourself.

Eastside County Park (5.2 acres)

A secluded sand beach, picnic tables and a pair of fire rings make this park worth the trip down the gravel road to get there. The park takes its name from its location on the eastern side of Washington Island.

Jackson Harbor Dunes Town Park (31.5 acres)

The docking facilities at Jackson Harbor Park are home port to many of the island's commercial fishing operations, and this pier has a distinctive "salty" appeal. The sand beach is an inviting place to swim. Changing houses are available. A hiking trail crossing the adjacent sand dunes provides an outstanding natural classroom. The Nature Conservancy has been instrumental in protecting this area and recently a critical parcel has been added to this preserve (listed separately).

Schoolhouse Beach Town Park (34 acres)

This town park once served as the Washington Island campground, but now the smooth stone beach and beautiful view of Washington Harbor are its chief attractions. A swimming raft is anchored offshore but this beach is best utilized by experienced swimmers since the water becomes quite deep just offshore. The park is well marked off Jackson Harbor Road.

Mountain Road Town Park (5 acres)

A heart-pounding climb provides an excellent view of Washington Island from an observation tower atop the mountain that gives this park its name. A newly constructed staircase leads to an observation tower. This climb is not for the faint of heart, but those with stamina will be rewarded with a fine vista.

PRESERVES

Jackson Harbor Ridges

Located at Jackson Harbor on Washington Island. Owned by the town of Washington Island and managed by the Washington Island Natural Area Board, this preserve was protected with assistance from the Nature Conservancy. For more information write: Arni Richter, Washington Island, WI 54246. Phone: 920-847-2296.

RECREATION:

The park is open year-round for hiking, nature study and photography.

This unique preserve encompasses an incredible diversity of natural communities including lake dunes and ridges, limestone sand flats and conifer forest. The

Nature Conservancy says the rare combination of ecosystems that are part of Jackson Harbor Ridges makes this the only beach of its kind known on the islands surrounding the Door Peninsula.

Cool, moist Lake Michigan breezes create a climate here conducive to the growth of rare plant species such as dwarf lake iris and arctic primrose. The beach gives way to a stand of pine trees and the site provides an outstanding view of Jackson Harbor. The wet upland forest is home to white cedar, fir and spruce trees. The Nature Conservancy says hikers also should be on the lookout for other plant species including shrubby St. John's-wort, dune goldenrod and prairie sand reed along the ridges and dunes of Jackson Harbor.

Protection of Jackson Harbor Ridges began in 1972. The town of Washington Island, assisted by the Nature Conservancy, purchased 42 acres that year along the southern boundary of Jackson Harbor, creating a public nature preserve. In 1988, the Nature Conservancy added a 43-acre tract adjacent to the original parcel.

Today, Jackson Harbor Ridges is an 85-acre natural area with 27 acres devoted to "biological and wildlife study, photography and 'careful walking,' " so plan your low-impact visit accordingly.

After arriving at Detroit Harbor aboard the Washington Island Ferry, head north along County W to Jackson Harbor. Turn off at Rock Island Road to Sunrise Road. Turn left at Sunrise Road and watch for the preserve just as the road bends right (east). Jackson Harbor Ridges is bordered by Town of Washington Island parkland to the west, but private property to the east along Sunrise Road. Please avoid trespassing.

BEACHES

Washington Island Sand Dunes

Deep, enchanting sand dunes cushion beach blankets on Washington Island's public beach. Because Washington Island is frequently fanned by cool Lake Michigan winds, the dunes provide a warm place to escape the breeze and absorb the heat of the sand on a sunny summer day. The island dunes also provide a grand view of Detroit Island and Lake Michigan.

From Detroit Harbor, take County W briefly to Detroit Harbor Road and turn right (east). Follow Detroit Harbor Road to County W until it becomes South Shore Drive about one mile from Washington Island Sand Dunes.

Eastside County Park Beach
The sand beach at Eastside County Park provides a nice place to beat the heat when other island beaches are beginning to get a little crowded. You'll have to travel across a gravel road to get to this one.

Jackson Harbor Beach
With Rock Island before you and the Jackson Harbor Dunes behind you it's tough to imagine a better location from which to enjoy a sunny day. Changing stations are available and the beach is a great place to absorb the rays while you wait to board the Karfi for a trip to Rock Island.

Schoolhouse Beach
The smooth pebble stones at Schoolhouse Beach are no substitute for sand, but the grand view of Washington Harbor and the swimming raft still attract plenty of visitors. This beach is not well suited for small children or poor swimmers, but those with experience in water will enjoy a visit.

Rock Island Beach
This beach conjures up images of Robinson Crusoe. Its magnificent isolation insures plenty of comfort. Sand dunes form a stunning backdrop and waves often provide opportunities for body surfing. A frequent breeze can chill a swimmer, but in July it's tough to resist frolicking in the surf.

Take the Washington Island Ferry from the Northport Dock to Detroit Harbor. Drive, bike, hitch-hike or take an island taxi to Jackson Harbor. Board the passenger ferry Karfi for the ten-minute crossing to

Rock Island. The beach is on the southeast side of the island, adjacent to the campsites.

BICYCLE TOURS

Washington Island Wheeling
(15 miles, 21 miles with sidetracks)

This tour follows paved roads through the heart of the island. There are opportunities to swim, sightsee and picnic as you travel from Detroit Harbor to Jackson Harbor amid the forests and fields of Washington Island.

Begin the tour as you depart the Washington Island Ferry. Heading up Point Lobdell Road you'll enjoy the wide shoulders and scenic forest as you make your way the 1.8 miles to the intersection with Main Road. Turn left on Main Road and you'll be pedaling into the island's "downtown" district, passing the island school, grocery store and community center. When you reach the Island Art and Nature Center at Jackson Harbor Road, you can either take the 3.6-mile round-trip sidetrack to Little Lake and the Jacobsen Museum or turn right on Jackson Harbor Road. A short jaunt off Jackson Harbor Road leads to Schoolhouse Beach. The smooth pebble beach here provides swimming opportunities and the view of Washington Harbor is worth the side trip even if you don't plan to take a dip. Continuing you'll pass the Washington Island Farm Museum before you reach the intersection with Mountain Road. A two-mile round-trip sidetrack down Mountain Road takes you to Mountain Lookout Town Park. A wooden staircase leads to an observation tower providing a sweeping view of the surrounding countryside. Backtrack to Jackson Harbor Road and continue past Sievers Looms and School to Jackson Harbor. You can catch the Karfi to Rock Island if you wish or explore the dunes and boreal forest of Jackson Harbor Ridges. Backtrack on Jackson Harbor Road to Deer Lane Road and turn left. This narrow road is tailor-made for bicycling. Continue to Lakeview Road and turn right. Proceed to Range Line Road and turn left. Range Line Road intersects with Detroit Harbor Road which will intersect with Point Lobdell Road for the trip back to the ferry dock. If you've got a little extra energy and are up for a swim, continue straight

WASHINGTON
ISLAND
WHEELING
BICYCLE TOUR

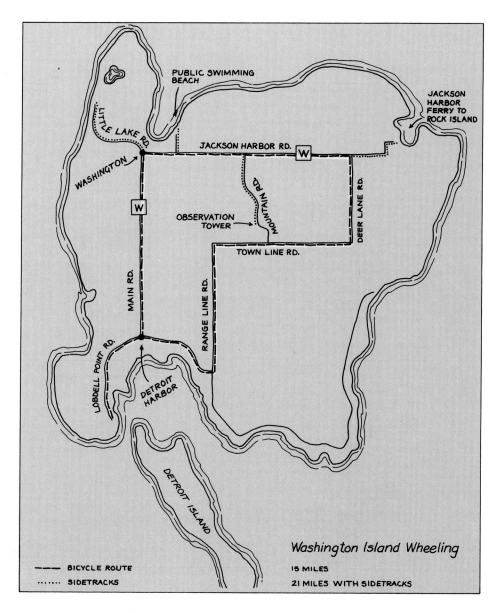

Washington Island Wheeling

——— BICYCLE ROUTE
······· SIDETRACKS

15 MILES
21 MILES WITH SIDETRACKS

on Range Line Road past Aznoe Road and turn left on South Shore Drive. South Shore Drive is paved up to Sand Dunes Public Beach. Here you'll find the finest swimming the island has to offer.

CANOE AND KAYAK ROUTES

Death's Door Passage

Death's Door translates from the French name for this strait, "Porte des Morts." Passage today can be an uneventful cruise aboard the Washington Island Ferry, or a major expedition undertaken by expert sea kayakers. Even in promising weather, this seven-mile crossing should not be taken lightly. Currents are unpredictable in the passage and swells, invisible from shore, often become steep and threatening. Plum Island in the middle of Death's Door can provide needed refuge during an emergency, but camping is prohibited. A manned Coast Guard station on the island once provided reassurance for paddlers but after more than one hundred years these operations were moved to Washington Island. The sight of the car ferry chugging through the strait may give kaykers some relief but it's often difficult for the ferry captains to see kayakers so be sure to give them a wide berth.

Rock Island State Park, off Washington Island's northeast shore, is a favorite destination of sea kayakers, making for a long day of paddling. Only a handful of paddlers successfully challenge this crossing each summer, but those who do enjoy rewards few others will ever know. To get to the put-in at the Northport Dock, take Highway 42 east of Gills Rock to the tip of the peninsula. Navigation chart: NOAA #14909.

Little Lake

Carry-in public access to Little Lake is available next to the Jacobsen Museum, reached via Main and Little Lake roads.

You'll be glad you car-topped your canoe for the ferry ride trip to Washington Island once you discover 24-acre Little Lake. Little Lake is a crystal-clear pool

210

located just a short way from Lake Michigan. Due to its limited development, you're likely to startle ducks, geese and herons as you paddle the marshy northwestern shoreline. The lake occupies a shallow bowl carved by glacial action and is separated from Lake Michigan by a cobblestone ridge. At normal water levels, Little Lake is a full three feet higher than Lake Michigan. The lake reaches a maximum depth of five feet and, because of winterkill, fishing is poor. Nevertheless, its near-pristine shoreline and clear waters combine to make lily dipping in Little Lake a simple pleasure. Even though you will be sorely tempted to do so, please avoid landing on the wooded shore. This is private property and the owners appreciate their privacy.

Rock Island Reefs

Kayakers willing to endure the expense of car topping their boats aboard the Washington Island Ferry can cross the dangerous Porte des Morts in comfort, safety and convenience. After arriving at Detroit Harbor, drive to Jackson Harbor where you'll find the Karfi loading passengers for the ten-minute ferry ride to Rock Island. The captain of the Karfi can advise kayakers of the conditions for the crossing to Rock Island, and, if necessary, shuttle your gear for a fee. Keeping the Karfi in sight will boost your confidence as you make your way to Rock Island. Be advised of the reefs separating Rock Island from Washington Island. Waves breaking over these shoals have caused the capsize of many a sea kayaker. Before setting up camp on Rock Island, you'll need to secure a permit from the ranger. Once on the island, paddling opportunities for circumnavigation are limitless, but beware of the weather. In this portion of the peninsula storms roll in quickly and can strike with a vengeance. During periods of fair weather, though, this is a lovely, blue open-water crossing for kayakers with intermediate skills and up. Navigation chart: NOAA #14909.

To get to the put-in at Jackson Harbor, leave the ferry dock on Washington Island by Point Lobdell Road. Turn left on Main Road to Jackson Harbor Road and turn right.

CITIES, TOWNS AND VILLAGES

Washington Island (pop. 550)

Washington Island rises from Lake Michigan using regal bluffs, stunning sand dunes and shady swamps to cast a magical spell on all who visit. The folks who call it home like to boast they live "north of the tension line," and visitors watching the ferry leave them behind are inclined to agree.

Today, getting to Washington Island is both safe and convenient aboard diesel-powered steel ships that routinely ply the Porte des Morts Strait. One hundred years ago the opposite was true. In fact, between 1872 and 1889 a lighthouse keeper on Pilot Island recorded an average of two shipwrecks a week in this area. Winter crossings have also taken their toll. In March of 1935, before the luxury of year-round ferry service, six young islanders returning by vehicle from the mainland put their trust in the winter ice. It was to be their final trip since the once-frozen strait had opened, sealing their fate.

Early Indian inhabitants of Washington Island not only feared the passage to the mainland, but also depended on it for protection from ambush by enemies. Archaeological explorations of the island have uncovered evidence of these early settlements and a window to their past.

The appeal of Washington Island lies in not only its isolation, but also its tempered climate. Influenced by the blue waters that surround it, the island remains cooler in the summer and warmer in the winter than its midwestern neighbors.

Outstanding fisheries drew the island's first white settlers and continue to attract tourists eager to battle salmon or trout aboard fishing charters that troll the island's 26 miles of shoreline. Door Peninsula historian Hjalmar Holand, never one to pass up a story even if it does sound a little fishy, tells of a 70-pound trout caught off Rock Island in 1860. Holand follows this tale with reports of a single fisherman netting 220 trout in just two days.

STRICT ZONING
Washington Island was the first township in Door County to adopt a strict zoning code. This has protected the island from over-development and assured that its scenic values will remain for future generations.

Woodcutters followed fishermen to Washington Island, finding that steamships laden with fish required fuel for the trip south. These hearty woodsmen were mostly Norwegians, Danes and Icelanders who began hammering out a living from the native timber. The influence of these native Scandinavians remains, and today the island is home to the oldest heritage of Icelandic ancestry in the United States.

Washington Islanders have always felt deeply attached to both their land and their neighbors. Environmental awareness has led to the creation of excellent parks, beaches and nature preserves with strict zoning laws assuring planned development. Community pride and cohesion is evident among local residents who support their summer baseball team with all the zest and loyalty of a major-league franchise. Many visitors choose to retire here, enjoying the safe, friendly atmosphere after discovering, as you may, that Washington Island is a great place to visit, but they'd rather live here.

Most visitors arrive aboard the Washington Island Ferry from Northport or Gills Rock. Some bring their private vessels and dock at either Detroit or Jackson harbors. A handful arrive by kayak, usually en route to Rock Island. And, the island also has a class A airport accommodating private airplanes.

Many visitors bring their own vehicles aboard the car ferry, enjoying the freedom while enduring the expense of personal transportation. Alternatives include taking an island tour train or renting a moped or a bicycle. Personal guided tours are also available.

Art and Nature Center: The center at the corner of Main and Jackson Harbor roads offers classes in art and nature. It's an excellent orientation spot for visitors. The center is open from the third week in June through September. A small admission is charged.

Washington Island Farm Museum: The museum offers a look at the history of farming on Washington Island. It's open from late May through October and admission is free.

ISLAND FESTIVITIES

Fireworks on the Fourth of July.

Fly-in fish boil on the third Sunday in July.

Scandinavian Festival on the first weekend in August.

Fireman's Ball on the second Saturday in August.

Fall Ball and Harvest Dinner on the second Saturday in October.

Sievers School of Fiber Arts: Weekend and week-long classes in spinning and weaving are offered here. The school is located on Jackson Harbor Road and offers dormitory-style lodging for students.

Library: The library is located off Lake View Road in the Community Center.

Jacobsen Museum: Located on the south shore of Little Lake, six miles from the ferry dock on the northwest corner of the island, the museum has a fine collection of natural and historic artifacts. It's open weekends from Memorial Day through mid-June, then daily through the summer. It is a great source of tourist information late in the season before it closes in mid-October.

Washington Island Chamber of Commerce: The address: Box 80, Washington Island, WI 54246; phone: 920-847-2225.

Sand Dunes Town Park: Access to the park is off South Shore Road about four miles east of the ferry dock. It has a great beach, and no crowds. Take the trail from the parking area up the hillside to the sand dunes and enjoy yourself. Four acres.

Schoolhouse Beach Town Park: This 34-acre park offers a marked swimming area with a raft for advanced swimmers. It's located five miles from the ferry dock on Washington Harbor, off Cemetery Road via Main and Jackson Harbor roads.

Eastside County Park: There's a great view of Hog Island, a national wildlife refuge for nesting herons, gulls and shorebirds, as well as picnic facilities here. Follow Lakeview Road to Lake Michigan.

Jackson Harbor Ridges: This nature preserve is not to be missed. The ridges here are actually sand dunes separated by low-lying depressions called swales. Endangered plants cling to life here, so plan a low-impact visit.

ISLAND DOCTOR
Washington Island has a resident doctor who keeps regular hours at the Washington Island Clinic. She is always on call for emergencies and urgent care. The island also has a team of trained Emergency Medical Technicians available for medical emergencies.

Mountain Road Town Park: Access to this five-acre park is off Mountain Road via Main and Jackson Harbor roads. A steep trail takes visitors to the summit of this 160-foot "mountain." An observation deck on top puts you above the trees for an island view.

Washington Island Recreation Center: Thanks to a one million dollar gift from John and Jane Mosling, Washington Island now boasts an indoor swimming pool, whirlpool, excerising room and community room. Completed in 1988, the 12,500 sqaure foot building is open to residents and visitors alike. Daily, vacation and annual passes are available. Write P.O. Box 66, Washington Island, WI 54246. Phone: 920-847-2226.

Washington Island Ferry Service

Gills Rock and Northport, both at the tip of the peninsula, are the two locations from which to launch your exploration of Washington Island. The two docks are served by competing commercial ferry operations. If you plan to bring your car to the island, you'll be departing from Northport, two miles east of Gills Rock at the end of Highway 42. If you plan to make the trip just to enjoy the scenery, or if you're bringing your bike for an island tour, you can save the expense of shuttling your car and board at either Gills Rock or Northport.

The trip from Gills Rock takes passengers aboard the *Yankee Clipper*. This 149-passenger ship, operated by Voight Marine Services, began operations in 1971. Captain Voight offers up to five round trips daily and affords a narrated crossing through Death's Door Passage from the last week in May through mid-October. Cost is about $7 round-trip and the *Yankee Clipper* doesn't charge for bicycles. You can combine this adventure with a guided tour of Washington Island aboard the Viking "Train" for an additional charge. For current fees and departure information phone: 920-854-2972.

A second vessel in the Voight fleet, the *Island Clipper*, sails Thursdays from mid-July to mid-August from Gills Rock to Fayette State Park on Michigan's Garden Peninsula. This all day, 34-mile trip takes one hour and 45 minutes each way and passes the historic Grand Traverse Island Chain before docking in Snail Harbor. During the three-hour stop at Fayette there are opportunities to tour the restored historic town site, swim and picnic. Sea kayakers have been known to make arrangements to be picked up or dropped off at Fayette when they're willing to challenge the spectacular crossing from Wisconsin to Michigan. The boat sails from late June through August and reservations are recommended. Cost is approximately $20 round-trip; phone: 920-854-2972.

ISLAND WILDLIFE
White-tailed deer, fox, raccoons, porcupine, skunk and a variety of waterfowl and birds call Washington Island home. There are no poisonous snakes or wolves on the island, and the only bear found here in recent years was relocated to the mainland once it became a nuisance at the town dump.

If you plan to bring your car to Washington Island, you'll be departing from the Northport Dock aboard ferries owned and operated by the Washington Island Ferry Service. Northport affords an ice-free passage to Washington Island in winter and shortens the trip from 45 to about 30 minutes in summer. Northport's summer residents protested moving the bulk of traffic from Gills Rock to this sleepy dock but were defeated by arguments made in the name of safety by the Washington Island Ferry Line. The car ferries serving Washington Island run year-round, regardless of weather. Occasionally, severe winds leave travelers stranded, but this is rare. Those prone to seasickness should take the necessary precautions since the trip can sometimes be a roller-coaster ride. Frequency of service depends upon the season. In winter when only one round trip is scheduled daily, automobile reservations are advisable. During July and August more than 20 round trips daily are offered, with weekend evening service available from mid-May through mid-August. If you plan to bring your car, you'll pay about $17 round-trip for the vehicle plus an additional $8 per person round-trip. Bicycles and kayaks are carried for $2.00 each. Boat trailers, recreational vehicles and campers are permitted to board for an additional fee. You must be in line at least ten minutes early. For current fees and precise departure information phone: 920-847-2546.

While the Washington Island Ferry Line is best known for serving residents and visitors of the island for which it is named, it has also come to the aid of stranded Sturgeon Bay residents. During November 1960, the Swedish ship *Carlsholm* rammed the city's downtown bridge. At the time, only a single bridge served Sturgeon Bay residents, and the accident threatened to isolate both sides of the city. Ferry line owner Arni Richter summoned his crews and brought the *Voyageur* and the *C. G. Richter* to Sturgeon Bay, running a 24-hour-a-day schedule for ten days until a temporary bridge was erected.

Gills Rock (pop. 75)

Gills Rock is best seen from the Washington Island Ferry as it approaches Garrett Bay and Hedgehog Harbor at the base of this New England-style village. Flanked by Death's Door Bluff to the west and Table Bluff to the east, Gills Rock has long been a haven for commercial fishermen earning their living amid the white-crested waves of Lake Michigan.

Porcupines are credited with naming Hedgehog Harbor. The story goes that Gills Rock pioneer Allen Bradley christened the harbor after discovering that his neighbor's boat had been gnawed by porcupines as it rested at Gills Rock over the winter.

Gills Rock today is considerably less chaotic than it was when automobiles waited in line to board the Washington Island Ferry. The end of the dock is a perfect place to enjoy a smoked fish snack if you can convince the gulls to find their own lunch. Winter is peaceful at this serene village, and as the waves crash and the ice builds on the dock, it's easy to forget it's time for the journey home.

Door County Maritime Museum: The museum is in Gills Rock at Wisconsin Bay Road and is open from Memorial Day to Labor Day. It features exhibits of marine artifacts and commercial fishing equipment.

Porte des Morts Town Park: There's a great view across Death's Door Passage from this small park (2.5 acres). There are also picnic facilities. The park is reached east of Gills Rock off Park Drive.

Gills Rock Memorial Park: This park features a ballpark, museum and picnic facilities. It's located in the village off Wisconsin Bay Road.

Gills Rock Advancement Association: Write for information at Gills Rock, WI 54210.

Northport (pop. 75)

A narrow, winding road through a forest grove brings visitors to the Northport Pier. Once a sleepy shoreside community of summer residents, Northport came to life when the Washington Island Ferry Line switched its operations from Gills Rock to the Northport Pier. Northport was the traditional landing site during the winter months and provided an alternative summer landing during strong northerly winds.

Improvements at the landing began in 1982, against the vocal protests of nearby property owners. A long court battle ensued and it wasn't until several years later that the courts ruled in favor of the ferry line allowing added development, including the addition of a restaurant at the landing.

While local property owners were stunned and disappointed by the decision, Washington Islanders were delighted. Not only does Northport provide an ice-free port in winter, it also reduces the crossing time to the island from 45 minutes to about 30 minutes.

EXPLORING SHIPWRECKS
There are about 120 shipwrecks surrounding Door County. Over fifty of these ships went down in the waters surrounding Washington and Rock Islands. In fact, the area is known as the graveyard of the Great Lakes. Scuba divers frequently dive these wrecks, occasionally making new discoveries. Shipwreck sites are protected and removing artifacts is not permitted.

(opposite page)
Resident waterfowl find safe haven at Gills Rock.

EPILOGUE
THE FUTURE

The legacy of the Door Peninsula is one of wild and beautiful shores, towering limestone cliffs and deep, aromatic forests. Its heritage is one of inquisitive explorers, self-reliant settlers and steadfast preservationists.

Over the years, ax has given way to bulldozer, meadows to condominiums and dirt roads to paved highways. Some call it progress; others, exploitation. Somewhere in between lies a delicate balance.

Door County's groundwater remains its most valuable and fragile natural resource. Land development, agriculture, road construction and urban sprawl threaten this water table. Left exposed by shallow soil and a limestone backbone, this resource is vulnerable to pesticide pollution, soil erosion and septic tank pollution.

Many critical ecosystems depend on this water for their continued existence. Dunes Lake Marsh north of Sturgeon Bay provides a striking example of this environment. This extensive, wild wetland is mostly swamp, marsh or ridge-swale topography. Donlan's Creek and its associated wetlands feed the lake, providing an important undisturbed home to wildlife and waterfowl. Shivering Sands Creek drains the marsh.

Also nearby is an area known locally as Cranberry Marsh. It consists of an extensive deep-water swamp and two shallow wilderness pools: Arbter and Schwartz Lakes. An upland forest separates the marsh from Lake Michigan. Combined, this large and complex ecosystem is perhaps the finest undeveloped roadless area on the peninsula.

Collectively, the Nature Conservancy has christened this region the Shivering Sands wetland complex. To its credit, the Conservancy is taking steps to protect this important resource for future generations. Its proximity to Whitefish Dunes State Park could make it a logical addition to this preserve. To date, its private owners have resisted developing the tract, but without permanent protection its unique character remains in jeopardy.

Other wetlands, including Coffey Swamp, a remote sedge bog on the north shore of Washington Island, the marshes on both ends of Kangaroo Lake, and the Lost Lake drainage area also provide critical habitat for insects, amphibians and waterfowl.

Creeks, streams and springs add to the peninsula's diverse fishery. Brook trout were once found in Logan, Hidden Spring, Keyes, Lilly Bay, Ephraim and Three Springs creeks. Today many of these creeks have been choked by road construction or drained for land development. Woodard, Stoney, Shivering Sands, Heins and Bear creeks support smelt runs. Game fish also spawn in these creeks and adjacent wetlands. It is up to us to assure that this natural cycle continues.

Early settlers were drawn to the Door Peninsula by its vast forests. Modern travelers arrive seeking the same commodity. Today about 8,000 acres of forest remain preserved in Door County parklands. The remaining woods are privately owned by commercial interests, farmers and recreational landowners. Unlike forests in some northern Wisconsin counties, the worth of Door Peninsula timber is measured not by its market price, but by its scenic value. Every effort to maintain these forests must be encouraged.

Door Peninsula residents have always had a deep appreciation for their trees and a strong desire to preserve them. Amid the forests of Glidden Drive, North Bay, Marshall's Point and the Black Ash Swamp are found maple, beech, basswood, birch, white pine, cedar and tamarack.

The grand vistas for which Door County is noted add a distinct aura to the peninsula. Viewed from the surrounding water these undeveloped bluffs provide a wonderful buffer of green space from developed areas nearby.

Today, however, escarpment forests are threatened. Development has already begun on the three-mile-long Egg Harbor escarpment. At the tip of the peninsula, Death's Door Bluff remains an important geographic landmark and prime habitat for rare cliff-dwelling plants. The bluff summit is covered by second-growth beech-maple while its terraced, moist cliffs are forested with white cedars. On Washington Island, Boyers Bluff towers above Lake Michigan. Its shaded cliffs and 200-acre upland forest remain rich in plant diversity.

Door Peninsula beaches have always attracted attention. Today, pressure is greater than ever to permanently alter the shoreline. Fish spawning sites are threatened by marinas. Shoreline forests are threatened by development and beaches are threatened by pollution.

But Door County has fared better than many other shoreside areas. Its landowners, visitors and leaders increasingly realize the value of a secluded beach and the importance of a forested sand dune.

While opinions vary as to what should be done to preserve the peninsula's natural beauty, there is much common ground.

To stave off the rapid development of farms, fields, woodlands and wetlands on the peninsula, a group of Door County landowners banded together in 1986 to form the Door County Land Trust, Inc. The goal of this nonprofit organization is to "preserve open space, and to protect the unique character and traditional way of life on the peninsula." Convinced that state and local land-use controls alone can not stem the tide of development, this local organization advocates private initiative in the form of land conservation easements.

Filed at the courthouse, these easements take the form of permanent deed restrictions binding both the present and the future owners of the property to limiting development or encouraging continued agricultural use. It does not change ownership of the land, and the property can still be sold or left to heirs.

Eighteen landowners have set aside over 600 acres, permanently protecting them, and ensuring the preservation of the Trust. For more information contact: Door County Land Trust, Inc., Box 345, Ephraim, WI 54211.

Another group on the front line of peninsula environmental action is the Door County Environmental

Council. This Fish Creek-based group acts as the watchdog of the peninsula. For more information contact: Door County Environmental Council, Fish Creek, WI 54212.

As the value of Door County waterfront property continues to spiral, the people of Wisconsin increasingly recognize this is their last chance to preserve undeveloped shoreline. By setting aside tax dollars to purchase property in the Baileys Harbor Boreal Forest Natural Area, the citizenry helps ensure the joys of a cobblestone beach, a blooming orchid and a cool dark woodland will be passed on to future generations.

The Nature Conservancy of Wisconsin and its Door Peninsula office have been instrumental in preserving the biological diversity of Door County. Projects currently under way at North Bay, Mink River, Shivering Sands wetland and Kangaroo Lake are aimed at preserving the most valuable and fragile natural areas of the peninsula. These remote and diverse biological areas harbor the soul of Door County where ospreys nest and black bears hide.

Those who love Door County find that the forests, beaches, bluffs and wetlands serve to sooth and inspire. To us, the loss of any of these diverse resources alter not only the landscape but also our lives.

No place can remain the same forever. Change adds vitality to this rugged peninsula. It creates jobs and adds to the quality of life. But it is clear there must be planned, orderly land management. What is wild must remain wild. What is indigenous must be allowed to thrive. What is pristine must not be destroyed. The future of Door County depends on us.

PO-SHO
Potawatomi Indian word meaning good-bye.

Po Sho
Craig Charles